# EINSTEIN AND MODERN FRENCH DRAMA

## An Analogy

## Kenneth Steele White

UNIVERSITY
PRESS OF
AMERICA

To Peace

## DEDICATION

Invaluable information on physics
was given to me by my father,
Dr. Marsh W. White. I want to
express my gratitude for his
assistance.

iii

## TABLE OF CONTENTS

# INTRODUCTION

[See the Synopsis]

Be warlike, says ignorance. Not so. Man is made for approximation to the Cosmic. The Cosmic is not warfare, but the mysteries of order.

Einstein said, "The most beautiful thing we can experience is the mysterious." (What I Believe, 1930). "It is the source of all true art and science."

Einstein once remarked, "It is a magnificent feeling to recognize the unity of a complex of phenomena which appear to be things quite apart from the direct visible truth."[1]

Thus Einstein, in simple language, told us a truth we must not forget. Art and science join in a search for elemental mystery, root of all human knowledge.

Artistic and scientific creativity are twins. They are indissoluble. Their final aims, not totally similar, have many affinities.

Strangely, we have overlooked the importance of these affinities. It is true that scientists have had vital roles in devising nuclear and hydrogen bombs, now the neutron bomb. The U.S. Government has rewarded them. A few writers, composers, musicians, dancers, actors, or choreographers have been given such high esteem. Most often, the art/science twins have separated. A scattered few have understood the interrelatedness of artistic and scientific discovery. Yet it exists.

---

[1] Quoted by Carl Seelig in Albert Einstein: A Documentary Biography, (London, 1956), p. 53.

French playwrights, from Alfred Jarry (1896) to Eugène Ionesco and Samuel Beckett (the 1950's onward), have in different ways insinuated the inextricability of knowledge, the eye's inner scrutiny of the multifarious personality, the dramatist's unique vantage point toward cosmic uncertainties.

Are these theatrical mysteries of the (1961) universe (as revealed in Ionesco's explosive La Colère) the identical, basic conundrums studied by physicists like Einstein? Why should they not be? We must be careful to distinguish the scientists' vocabulary (special or general relativity, space-time, the Döppler effect) from the metaphors employed by a playwright. Metaphorically, Ionesco blows up our entire planet in La Colère: prescient or blind? Hasty, inordinately hasty, or prophetic of a real collapse of the cosmos billions of years from now? In any sense scientific?

Vocabulary is vital. When a physicist says "energy" or "force," he attaches very specific meanings to the terms. Some men in physics refuse to allow non-scientists to appropriate such words in unscientific ways.

Science and the humanities ultimately focus on nature and human nature from different angles of perspective. At root, studies lead to somewhat analogous conclusions. A physicist exploring the phenomena of mass and energy of a projectile finds exact measurements. When an automobile, travelling a very high speed, runs into an abutment and the driver is killed, humanities try to discover the reasons and effects of the driver's folly. They, along with scientists, must decide on what physical consequences the car had; but their basic study is concentrated on what happened morally or mentally to the unfortunate driver so that he touched death. Death is the final element; humanist and scientist cannot escape that; it must be understood, accepted.

Where precisely is Einstein's "unity"? In a complex of phenomena, he asserts, the direct, visible truth may be hidden by apparent contradictions. He finds it magnificent to pursue some species of unity, nevertheless. This question, one of science's most difficult, similarly tantalizes humanists. Drama probes into it deeply; so do ballet, sculpture, painting, orchestral music, poetry, literature.

Realizing mysterious unity, sung by poets like Baudelaire since the nineteenth century, and many before Baudelaire, is the aim of humanities as well as sciences. The avenues taken by each are logically analogous, if only at times.

"Consider anything, only don't cry!" writes Lewis Carroll in Through the Looking Glass.

Modern science and French dramaturgy since 1896 have made bold to sight at almost everything--including in the theatre the experimental explosion of the nuclear bomb, wrecking the lives of Japanese fishermen (Gabriel Cousin, Le drame du Fukuruyu-Maru) (1960) and the ultimate disintegration of the world (Ionesco, La Colère), total atomic warfare shattering the planet.

"Don't cry!" is a wry command. Carroll meant to advise: "Don't be shocked at the world's folly." More has happened in the last century in physics than in the whole sweep of history. Other disciplines and human endeavors follow closely in this incredible path. In truth, we are overwhelmed. The world is too much with us. Plethora. Superabundance of complication. Complexity. Stress. Anguish and anxiety. We know these too well. Claustrophobia. Paranoia. Schizoid and manic-depressive reactions. Since 1896, and especially since the Second World War, these exacerbated states have been legion. Divorce has proliferated; in the United States, nearly half of all marriages now end in divorce.

Scientists, Einstein in particular, have been courageous. When startled or frightened by their findings, they have not recoiled. Our modern, technological age is the result. Medicine cures previously impossible diseases. Polio has almost disappeared. New viruses, new diseases always pop out. In physics, astounding discoveries have been preludes for exploration of outer space, Neptune, Jupiter being visible in their spectacular girths. The realm of physics has leap-frogged via astrophysics and other branches to encompass the cosmic structure as giant telescopes and other methods study it.

Einstein's amazing hypotheses shattered precedents. Newton was partly eclipsed. Einstein gave to human knowledge radical new information about mass, curvature of space, matter-energy distribution, how light travels,

ix

speed of light, the geometry of space, and gravitational interrelationships.

No single playwright can be compared by analogy to Einstein. In France, Ionesco and Beckett were leaders. The Swiss-German, Friedrich Dürrenmatt offered an unforgettable drama of physicists and atomic secrets, The Physicists (1962). A play of foreboding accuracy, The Physicists presents a trio of enigmatic scientists who hold the keys to the world's atomic future. Are they half-mad or mad? The play is a masterpiece of structure, character-painting, and intrigue; it deserves to be better known.

Mark Twain wrote, "There is something fascinating about science. One gets such wholesale returns out of such a trifling investment of fact."[2]

No longer true, though an incisive quip. Mark Twain's humor ran loose. An opposing point of view often pertains. Scientific data are abundant, everywhere. There is too much science, many humanists would claim. Einsteinian findings and conjectures, world-renowned, now and then outshone even the best work in the humanities.

The laws of physics have to be statistical in character. Not so the principles of drama. This wide gap, as fundamental as anything possible in a comparative study, is a problem. I do not intend to come anywhere near bridging the chasm. This would be fallacious. Drama and physics participate in the essential: all Nature and all human striving. Analogies are feasible. Laws of each discipline vary drastically. I will not infringe on these laws. A bridge is a need today. I will attempt to locate it.

"The world is out of joint." Metaphysical dramas since 1945, especially the dour, far-seeing plays by Samuel Beckett (Waiting for Godot, Endgame, Krapp's Last Tape, Happy Days, Comédie, Actes divers) have plunged the theatre-going public into consternation. Beckett is a philosophical mystifier. His perceptual

---

2 Quoted in B. K. Ridley, Time, Space and Things (Harmondsworth: Penguin, 1976), p. 10.

angles are well-nigh unknown.  In Godot, his now-famous
bums, Estragon and Vladimir, represent lost inhabitants
of this earth, hoping that diversions can be found to
pass the time.  Time, that elixir the prediction of
which can never be tasted.  Beckett's cosmos is indeed
close to inscrutability.  Strangely, he confessed to a
friend, Peggy Guggenheim, that he had a compelling desire to return to his mother's womb.  Womb-like in gigantic scope, his universe refuses to welcome, to give
solace.  Is Beckett's "womb" analogous to Einstein's
closed universe?  On the surface, such a presupposition
could seem foolhardy.

From Dante, whom he admired, Beckett inherited a
special darkness of the soul.  In fact, Endgame (1957)
and its overbearing suffocation (a chess game of life
and death hovering upon conclusion) are almost entirely
somber.  No hope of changing the drift into moribund
forgetfulness.  No hope.  Death is the main character.
Life has been all but squelched.  Life is surfeited;
there has been too much living.  Hyperbole, nihilism,
overstatement.  Beckett could hardly go farther.

Says Hamm:  "I'll give you nothing more to eat."
Clov:  "Then we'll die."  Hamm..:  "I'll give you just
enough to keep you from dying.  You'll be hungry all
the time."[3]

In ritual preparation (Hamm orders Clov to go and
get a mysterious sheet), the play, snail-like, advances.
Its goal overtakes all else.  It is death.  Only Beckett
could have written such a play, a gageure.  It reeks,
in metaphysics and simple human compassion, of a never-
never land, life-end stasis.

Why should a playwright such as Beckett have e-
merged as the Nobel prize winner in 1969?  Beckett had
participated with the French Resistance in World War II.
Waiting for Godot reflected in part his anguish at
perilous waiting.  German soldiers in force, reported
to be nearby, could endanger his life and those of his
friends.  The drama's fiber is bold.  Godot may never
appear; but courage in waiting is what makes each day
toll.

_____

3 Samuel Beckett, Endgame (New York: Grove Press,
1958), p. 5.

xi

Thus the moment, the early 1950's, was propitious for a dramatist of Beckett's envergure. No one wrote like him. His strength was vision of an unworldly non-universe peopled by bums, little people, outcasts. Hope is not his strong point. Resistance is.

Whether or not there are similarities between Einstein's radically new cosmos and Beckett's implied nearly-non-world must be examined. Paradoxes float. So do contradictions. Yet one fact is clear. Einstein and Beckett shared a deep apprehension of the menace of atom bombs in our world. Beckett's works postdate the launching of the first experimental nuclear bomb. Einstein had promulgated his prophetic special and general theories of relativity long before, some thirty years in advance of Hiroshima dnd Nagasaki.

Albert Einstein, with Alexander Friedmann, predicted that the universe itself is and will be dynamic and expanding. One of the results of Einstein's thinking was the concept that collapse of the cosmos is inevitable. In the universe, everything can ultimately change, mutate. As Einstein saw it, the universe is closed. Space is curved. Light rays curve imperceptibly.

Cosmic uncertainty, peril, and a principal fear, fright of death, even when bathed in the sun's radiance, inhabited Ionesco's mind together. Amazed and awed at the unimaginable radiance of the sun's light, Eugène Ionesco reacted by musing on the infinite. Overwhelmed by the immense ocean of the infinite, he was indelibly marked by the brilliant sunlight of existence:

> When my lieutenant and my boss are back in their rooms, they could, for example, just like me, being outside the social order, be nightmares, and having stripped off their social personality, suddenly find themselves naked, like a body stretched out on the sand, amazed to be there and amazed at their own amazement, amazed at their own awareness as they are confronted with the immense ocean of the infinite, alone in the brilliant, inconceivable and indisputable sunlight of existence.[4]

---

[4] Eugène Ionesco. Notes and Counternotes, (New York: Grove, 1974), p. 108.

Physics is about the simple things of the universe, Ridley has asserted.[5]

Many down-to-earth, amateur analysts of physics might demur. Einstein himself once declared that if he had the power to change anything in his lifestyle, he would have written so simply that every layman could follow. Simplicity is a key issue. In literature as in physics, the simplest germ of expression is valued. Samuel Beckett, in his deceptive candor and colloquialism in Waiting for Godot, as in Endgame, hid depths of profundity and nuance.

In Einstein's theory of general relativity, the basic principle is that the laws of physics should be the same for accelerated observers and hence, by the principle of equivalence, for all observers in whatever gravitational field they happen to be in. In particular, the velocity of light remains a constant, and light travels in straight lines, unless distorted by the presence of a gravitational body. The curvature of space is directly related to the matter--energy--distribution. In this way the geometry of space, itself of necessity universal, is intimately related to another universal thing--gravitation.[6]

The title of this essay may shock: "Einstein and Modern French Drama: an Analogy." Understandably. Two seemingly dissimilar forms of creativity cannot be tightly paired. Bridging the difference is perilous. In fact, it cannot be bridged in entirety. The technique I propose is analogy. Distant analogy, sometimes, yet more than provocative in its newness. Analogy may touch upon affinity. Ionesco's visions of cosmic explosion do contain a significant affinity with Einstein's foreshadowings of atomic energy, which was soon to produce nuclear and hydrogen bombs.

---

[5] B. K. Ridley. Time, Space and Things (Harmondsworth: Penguin, 1976), p. 11.

[6] Ridley, Ibid., pp. 128-129.

Space exploration, implicit in Einsteinian concepts of space-time and the speed of light, has fur-
nished the topic for a number of modern dramas, including Armand Gatti's Chroniques d'une planète provi-
soire (1962).

Gatti's play is a-scientific. He scrutinizes not
the exploration of esoteric space, but man's actions
when "liberated" on a new planet. Gatti is political,
far to the left. Politics overtake dramatic humanity.

Einstein, in his social thought, devoted much of
his later life to Zionism and the search for formulae
for world peace. Gatti's aim is peace for the prole-
tariat and by extension for everyone. Disillusionment
seeps into his drama. Such discouragement was not
foreign to Einstein, who near the end of his life was
one of the best-known figures in the world, having
fought the impossible struggle for peace in our time.

Giraudoux provided a distant analogue. In The
Madwoman of Chaillot (1945), a delicious satire on
modern potentates who seek to ravage the earth's oil,
Giraudoux implies the end of the world as we know it,
the world of graciousness, warm love, gentility, and
charm. The "mecs," the super-operators who are avid
to control everything (pre-EXXON and TEXACO) embody
the future: ruthlessness, selfishness, exploitation,
death of everybody once oil has been depleted.

Einstein by implication forecast atomic transmuta-
tion (its concomitant being world destruction); Giraudoux saw ahead to the moment when bandits on the trail
of world oil would impoverish the subjugated earth. Two
world finales, different yet strangely analogous.

Samuel Beckett's world peters out interminably. In
Waiting for Godot, Vladimir and Estragon, the bums, with
Pozzo and Lucky, the interlopers, are doomed to the same
fate. Timeless Time. No gulf, it cannot swallow them
up. A vortex running forever. Is this the end? Life's
succulence is over. No atomic fragments in any literal
sense, Vladimir and Estragon are nonetheless bits and
flotsam to be forever whirled in the pool of a species
of pseudo-life. From Beckett to Einstein, the vortex of
timeless time, a spin on the wings of critical imagination is not an impossible journey.

Ironic half-travesty of Einstein, Friedrich Dürren-

matt's The Physicists elects worlds of fantasy to escape real dangers of being tracked down by foreign
powers gluttonous for atomic secrets possessed by the
play's heroes.

One semi-mad scientist calls himself Einstein:

> I am Einstein. Professor Albert Einstein.
> Born the 14th of March, 1879, at Ulm. . .
> It was I who evolved the formula $E=mc^2$, the
> key to the transformation of matter into
> energy. I love my fellow men and I love my
> violin, but it was on my recommendation
> that they built the atomic bomb. (...He
> rises and goes into his room. He is heard
> fiddling. Kreisler. Liebesleid.)[7]

Dürrenmatt, like many playwrights of his period,
was hypnotized by the unheard-of power of the nuclear
bomb. Through a quasi-madman, he portrayed Einstein as
the virtual father of atomic warfare, overlooking his
assiduous quest for peace.

The great paradox of Einstein is here. Proponent
of pacific solutions to the world's conflicts, the physicist had told President Roosevelt in a letter (which
he often said he regretted) that plans for the nuclear
bomb should be carried through.

Apocalyptic and semi-apocalyptic ends to our cosmos
were foreseen in two little-known French dramas, Georges
Schehadé's Les Violettes[8] and Gabriel Cousin's Le drame
du Fukuryu-Maru.[9]

From the essence of violets, a cracked scientist
concocts a powerful substance capable of blowing up the
entire universe. Romance rears its head. Before he
can accomplish his task, he is prevented from doing it
by a lover. Helas, the secret is known to others.
While his head is turned by love, others take the secret

---

7 Dürrenmatt, The Physicists, (New York Grove, 1962),
Act II, p. 93.

8 Georges Schehadé, Les Violettes (Paris: Gallimard,
1960).

9 Gabriel Cousin, Le drame du Fukuryu-Maru (Paris:
Gallimard, 1960).

and turn it into a dastardly usage: a gigantic explosion threatening the world.

The fate of Les Violettes had much in common with other French and German plays warning of the potential shattering of the world by atomic bombs. It had little repercussion. Why? It seems certain that spectators were not prepared to face the idea that the entire universe might one day blow up in our faces. Total fear is unbearable. We shy away; we pretend that the totality of menace is simply not there.

Gabriel Cousin's Le drame du Fukuryu-Maru is flawed but overwhelming. Japanese fishermen and peasants sing folk songs as they prepare to launch their large fishing ship on an expedition. Wives say fond farewells; sweethearts knot relationships with departing sailors. A colorful panorama of a Japanese fishing village and dock area is essayed, with some success. Fraught with irony, the farewells are full of doom.

A strange hail falls on the fishing ship. It is fallout from an American atomic test.

Results are almost immediately catastrophic. Skin falls off; noses are eaten; strange maladies come about. When the ship returns to its native port, laments greet the disfigured sailors. No one more than Cousin has captured the pathos and horror of atomic fallout, possible plague of our era.

Le drame du Fukuryu-Maru was based on an actual catastrophe in the South Seas. The Japanese fishing ship was apparently not warned in time. The American test explosion and fallout proceeded with no regard for fishermen's lives. Harbinger of a future loaded with danger for all those in the path of fallout...

Even the French, who opposed American tests in the Pacific during the early years of testing, could not stomach Le drame du Fukuryu-Maru. Too stark, too horrendous. Rarely, if ever, has the drama been produced in the United States. Its ringing authenticity is unique.

# CHAPTER I

Certain laws of physics imply strong dramatic impact. They may seem dry. When we seek to comprehend the full import of these laws, ordinary illustrations, however humble, help to clarify. Everyday "relativity," which differs from that of physics itself, provides many an example.

Depending on specific conditions, sight of a given object varies radically relative to the observer. I see a moving airplane from a vertical angle; you see it from a 45 degree angle; we would describe its speed quite differently. Above us, it looks fast; far away, it seems to be going very slowly.

Seen from the end zone farthest away from the ball, a halfback circling left end appears to be travelling mostly to his left; observed from the forty-yard line high in the stands, his forward progress is much clearer. A movie starlet (Bo Derek) has great appeal to a twenty-year-old who likes her particular style; to a fifty-year-old, she is overdone and artificial. Not only age, but emotional set determine our definitions of a Hollywood actress.

The very nature of an object depends on relativity, as we ordinarily think of it, without reference to physics. Watched through venetian blinds, part of an apartment building may strike us as being a prison turret.

Einstein, in a wholehearted effort to awaken the mind of the common man, always wanted to write with simplicity. He did not achieve this. Einstein's ideas are basically simple, though his language is not. Those of us who are not scientists are often befuddled by the subtle and complicated world he described. The beauty of his theories is simplicity. Einstein was a physicist who relentlessly tried to simplify his ideas.

Like Spinoza, Einstein found it impossible to imagine anything like nothingness before the beginning. "God is subtle but he is not malicious," stated Einstein in one of his most famous pronouncements. Therefore the great physicist believed in a God who did not maliciously punish the inhabitants of our world for their mis-

1

deeds. In long range, his statement has portentous prolongations: God's wisdom will not allow the cosmos to be obliterated by a gigantic nuclear bomb explosion, nor man to be wiped off the face of the earth. More subtle, more intricate measures will be part of our destiny. Not total annihilation.

What is certain? This is one of the great problems of physics. Can we predict? The layman believes naively that science forecasts accurately, even certainly.

A leading concept in modern science is that of Werner Heisenberg, German winner of the 1932 Nobel Prize in physics: the uncertainty principle, also named the indeterminacy principle. This has vast repercussions, and by implication carries over into the reaches of modern drama.

Most simply stated, Heisenberg's principle is that it is not possible to tell with certainty both the velocity of a subatomic particle and its location at the same time. In other words, absolute scientific accuracy concerning speed and placement is impossible.

"It is impossible to determine with arbitrarily high accuracy both the position and momentum (essentially velocity) of a subatomic particle like the electron.
The effect of this principle is to convert the laws of physics into statements about relative probabilities instead of absolute certainties.[1]

The ramifications of Heisenberg's principle are clearly of the first importance. Relative probabilities are Einstein's forte. If a basic element of the physical world is uncertain and unpredictable, what of human conduct and all the arts? They seem to follow the same law, indeterminate in any absolute sense. Few con-

---

[1] The New Columbia Encyclopedia, eds. William H. Harris and Judith S. Levey (New York: Columbia University Press, 1975), p. 1217.

cepts from the sciences have gone more deeply into the wellsprings of human nature and his relationships with the cosmos.

Why are measurements of subatomic particles in physics uncertain? The answer is unusually significant. When any system is measured, it must be disturbed. Less than perfect precision in measurement is the result.

Analogies of this finding as they are seen in literature, and especially in modern French theatre, are manifold. Relative accuracy may be a prime feature of literary characterization and plot, as well as of language itself. This has long been accepted in literary criticism; but how many people are willing to admit that physics and other sciences are dominated by indeterminacy, or more simply by the impossibility of totally accurate predictability?

Here is a basic premise of my book. Heisenberg's principle and Einstein's relativity, together, tell us unmistakably that prediction and predictability have their risks. No one is capable of proclaiming a sure way to foresee what will happen next.

Of course, Heisenberg referred to subatomic particles. This is one level of physics. Einstein, whose most famous ideas investigated light, mass and energy, relativity and motion, gravitation and inertia, photoelectricity, and specific heat capacities, the motion of atoms, subatomic phenomena, and the quantum theory, had extraordinary versatility.

These scientific findings, of course, do not necessarily have parallels in the down-to-earth activities of John and Joan Smith in any country in the world. Some may. This bald statement must be proved. At the same time, what of playwrights' words on stage? Are they in any way parallel to these scientific precepts? If not totally parallel, are they contiguous? Do they touch or nearly touch somehow? I believe they do.

Is Heisenbergian uncertainty with subatomic particles in any way consistent with other types of uncertainty in human comportment? Again, I believe so. Einstein's relativity, a principle of pure physics, may have affinities in what we say and do. Let us seek them out.

"In gravitational fields there are no such things as rigid bodies with Euclidean properties: thus the fictitious rigid body of reference is of no avail in the general theory of relativity," wrote Einstein.[2]

Strictly realistic plays in France, in mid-nineteenth century until about 1910, evinced dramatic rigidity. Stringent lines of characterization (often unilinear, seldom complex), astringent, one-directional plots, unrelentingly literal language, all supposedly like life, reigned on serious Parisian stages. Middle-class problems were dramatized, sometimes sermonized: Emile Augier's Le Gendre de M. Poirier (1854), famous in its day, castigated the social institution of the courtesan and financial abuses. Family complications and divorce were other themes.

At the same time, Alexandre Dumas fils was denouncing adultery, prostitution, illegitimacy, hypocrisy, fraud, and other social ills on stage. He wrote thesis plays. There was no question of his point of view. Love was primary. He was doctrinaire, arbitrary. As S. A. Rhodes put it, "the stage became a pulpit, the play a dramatic sermon."[3]

His first triumph was La Dame aux Camelias (1852). In English, it is known as Camille. Verdi's world-famous opera, La Traviata, is based on this play. Love is the theme. Didacticism was Dumas fils' hallmark. In certain plays he used a raisonneur, an author's mouthpiece. Argumentation was rigid and pat; there was no possibility of artistic ambivalence. In plays, such rigidity was doomed to disappear in the best playwrights' work with the advent of the twentieth century.

Einstein's dismissal of "rigid bodies with Euclidean properties" was significant. In drama, if a play is indeed a creative, partial analogy to the construction of a scientific theory, its own type of rigidity,

---

2 Albert Einstein, Relativity: the Special and General Theory (New York: Crown, 1961), p. 98.

3 S. A. Rhodes, The Contemporary French Theater (New York: F. S. Crofts, 1947), p. 2.

reflecting beliefs of the society around it, tends to be a conviction which passes with time. Anything which is too brittle, too locked in temporality, can be shattered.

Naturalistic drama in France accentuated tendencies of the realistic plays which had preceded them. Naturalism vaunted the "slice of life" play. By 1865 the Goncourt brothers produced a first sketch of what was to be the naturalistic theatre. Henriette Maréchal (1863) was a failure. Alphonse Daudet had no more success with L'Arlésienne (1872). Emile Zola, not a great dramatist, contributed Thérèse Raquin, a drama of seedy milieux, in 1873.

In the Préface to Thérèse Raquin, Zola explained his goals:

> I am absolutely convinced that the naturalistic movement will soon assert itself in the theatre and will bring to it the power of reality, the new life of modern art. The experimental and scientific spirit of the century will spread to the theater, and therein lies the only possibility of renewal for our stage.[4]

Zola's statement rings clear. Science and experimentation, he predicts, will come into theatre. This was a tenet of naturalism. Sometimes overstated, very likely. It also has truth. Zola himself said frequently that Science was a master. In fact, Science, at the end of the nineteenth century, had assumed rights of hegemony. People looked up to Science as a new savior. Disillusionment slowly followed.

In the period just before Einstein, physics in the Euclidean pattern held that there were rigid bodies with Euclidean properties. After Einstein, such belief was impossible. Rigidity, in his concept, was banished. Once the Naturalists in France had had their day, this concept in drama was discredited. French theatre in the Zola mold had tried to follow Science rather stringently, at times naively. It was in a blind alley. Rigid adherence to "slices of life" had been a mistake.

---

4 Emile Zola, Préface to Thérèse Raquin, cited in S. A. Rhodes, Ibid., p. 2.

## CHAPTER II

In <u>Hamlet</u>, Shakespeare, in a famous speech, appears to equate figurative notions of Nature and of the Cosmos:

...nature cannot choose his origin
By the o'er growth of some complexion,
Oft breaking down the pales and forts of reason,
Or by some habit, that too much o'er-leavens
The form of plausible manners--that these men,
Carrying, I say, the stamp of one defect,
<u>Being nature's libery, or fortune's star,</u>
<u>His virtues else be they as pure as grace,</u>
As infinite as man may undergo,
Shall in the general censure take corruption
From that particular fault. The dram of evil
Doth all the noble substance to a doubt
Of his own scandal.[1]

<u>Fortune's star</u> is the clue. If man's destiny is linked to a partial cosmic apprehension of what he is doing on earth, the star of his fortune leads him unremittingly. The cosmos is in him. His potentially infinite virtues, ready to be stamped by defect, reflect cosmic potentialities. This is part of the greatness of <u>Hamlet</u>. Man goes beyond man.

Hamlet's sense of time matches Time and the world.

The time is out of joint; o cursed spite,
That ever I was born to set it right.[2]

Profoundly dramatic, this passage illustrates Hamlet's metaphysics. Why was he set on these lands, in Denmark, to put things right? What agency did it? Is it a curse? Why is the world out of joint?

Later, Hamlet, addressing Rosencrantz and Guildenstern, laments that the earth is "nothing to me but a foul and pestilent congregation of vapors." In this

---

[1] William Shakespeare, <u>Hamlet</u>, (ed. Francis Fergusson) (New York: Dell, 1960), Act I, sc. 4, p. 60.

[2] <u>Ibid.</u>, Act I, sc. 5, p. 73.

7

speech, one of the most important in the play, Hamlet compares man's nobility to dust.

> I have of late, but wherefore I know not, lost all my mirth, foregone all custom of exercises; and indeed it goes so heavily with my disposition, that this goodly frame the earth, seems to me a sterile promontory, this most excellent canopy the air, look you, this brave o'erhanging firmament, this majestical roof fretted with golden fire, why it appeareth to me nothing but a foul and pestilent congregation of vapours. What a piece of work is man, how noble in reason, how express and admirable in action, how like an angel in apprehension, how like a god--the beauty of the world; the paragon of animals; and yet to me, what is this quintessence of dust? Man delights not me; no nor woman neither, though by your smiling you seem to say so.[3]

The final uncertainties of science are here. Physics apprehends the cosmos temporarily and imperfectly. All is in change, flux. Is man in fact the paragon of animals or is he merely the quintessence of dust? The whole problem of human nature is called into question by Hamlet. His sardonic turn of mind classifies man on the lowest scale possible, not even animal-like. One of the summits of literature, Hamlet proves that an unscientific approximation of what is human reaches toward the o'erhanging firmament, cosmic glory. Poetry intimates images which science helps to construct.

Francis Fergusson has wisely said, "Shakespeare makes sure that the vision of hell or world's end that we get through (King Lear) shall be felt as utterly indigestible, an eternal pole of human experience opaque to reason."[4]

Scientific entropy is curiously unveiled when the blind Gloucester proclaims that in Lear is progressive, total ravaging as the world nears its end:

---

3 Ibid., Act II, sc. 2, pp. 94-95.

4 Francis Fergusson, "Introduction by the General Editor," Shakespeare's King Lear (New York: Dell, 1960), p. 13.

O ruined piece of nature; this great world
Shall so wear out to naught.[5]

King Lear's incarnation of world's end is a model.
It is ineluctable. It is indivisible. Francis Fergusson's pointed statements that our vision of Lear,
"opaque to reason," is an "eternal pole of human experience" are indicators. Lear's induced madness casts him
into a valley of semi-humanity from which he cannot escape.

The entropic model is comprehensive. As Lear
wears out, so the world. Lear is a model for Time's
plunderings. The partial scientific concept of entropy,
debated by the knowledgeable, takes literary shape in
Lear as an ultimate, all-absorbing metaphor.

Scurrilous and irreverent, Alfred Jarry's Ubu Roi
(Ubu the King), a pastiche of Shakespeare (Macbeth,
Julius Caesar, and possibly other dramas) startled the
theatrical world of Paris on December 10, 1896.

Jarry aimed his arrows into the absolute. For a
few instants, he succeeded. Greed. Avaraciousness.
Cupidity. Dreamworld revery. Bloodthirstiness. This
brash teenager from Brittany, who meant to mock a rotund
professor as well as Shakespeare's bloodlettings, created more than he had hoped. Ubu is a stentorian model
of carnage and stupidity, of cosmic uncertainty. Ubu
the King rollicks through murder as festivity, grand-
scale theft as diversion. Configuration in burlesque
fashion of man's fall from Grace, the farce pulls no
punches.

Father Ubu is the anti-hero. Grotesque, with a
swinging belly, he clamors. Deprived of a god, he wal-
lows sidewise toward eventual disaster. His fate is
sealed after multitudinous killings and a strange war on
a Napoleon-styled steppe in Lithuanian snow.

Less virulent than her husband, Mother Ubu still
sees him for what he is:

Sagouin toi-même! Qui m'a bati un animal
de cette sorte?

---

5 Ibid., Act IV, sc. 6, p. 177.

9

(Filthy so-and-so beast yourself! Who
ever devised an animal of this kind for me?")[6]

Ubu is indeed a quasi-animal. His conscience is
moribund. Quickly he becomes sheer rapacity. His cosmos is without guidance. No dictatorial God represses
him.

A final voyage overseas, undertaken by Ubu and con-
spirator friends without a capable helmsman or captain,
mocks man's rudderless shiftings in a world without cosmic framework. God appears only in spoutings, at times
blasphemous. Ubu the King, beneath wild surfaces of
murderous temptations, conveys serious forewarnings.
The modern era is about to begin. God has been thrown
aside. Science, a new, spurious god, cannot replace
true divinity. Science is virtually absent from the
farce. An emptiness remains. The twentieth century
dawns.


Le Soulier de Satin (The Satin Slipper),[7] by Paul
Claudel, was written in Paris and Tokyo in 1919 and 1924
and published in 1928-1929. It evokes the sixteenth
century: Spain, Bohemia, America, Morocco. Claudel,
who wanted to be a French Shakespeare, hurdles time and
space. His style is grandiloquent.

Claudel's dramatic language, which seeks nobility
of expression, gives temporal and spatial structure a
certain degree of firmness. Echos of Pirandello, whose
Six Characters in Search of an Author, was played by
the Pitoeffs in Paris in 1923, may be heard. There is
no unity of action, place, ambiance, or time. One
critic, Marcel Girard, has noticed an "esthetics of
ubiquity."[8] Claudel's vision is entirely Catholic.

---

6 Alfred Jarry, Ubu Roi, in Tout Ubu (Paris: Librairie Générale Française, 1962), Act II, p. 61.

7 Paul Claudel, Le Soulier de Satin (Marcel Girard,
  ed.) (Paris: Classiques Larousse, 1956).

8 Marcel Girard, in Ibid., Notice, p. 21.

The play's plot is double. Don Rodrigue and Dona
Prouhèze tumble into tragedy. Dona Musique and her fi-
ancé, the "Vice-Roi" of Naples, have an idyllic love.
The conquest of the world and its unity are the spring-
boards of dramatic action. Above this is the spiritual
play: the freeing of souls which have been held cap-
tive. Claudel rejects standard psychology. Providence
is his cornerstone.

Total theatre has roots in Claudel. Circus, cine-
ma, mime, dance, songs, vaudeville turns fill The Satin
Slipper. Claudel had an important role in opening the
French stage to these untraditional devices, freeing it
from nineteenth-century constraints.

Cosmic time, cosmic space. Claudel uses these notions. The hero, Don Rodrigue, incarnating atemporali-
ty, has thoughts only of Dona Prouhèze. He compares her
to his star:

(It is not only her eyes, it is she
quite entirely who is a star for me!)[9]

...

they showed me this queenly heavenly body,
this splendid star all by herself in
the diadem of transparent heaven...[10]

How I love these millions of things
which exist together! There is no soul
so wounded that the sight of this immense
concert does not awaken a weak melody in it![11]

Rodrigue states plainly that certain words of Dona
Prouhèze stop Time from existing:

...these words which stop the heart and
prevent time from existing![12]

---

[9] Ibid., Première Journée, sc. 7, p. 51.

[10] Ibid.

[11] Ibid., p. 53.

[12] Ibid.

11

Like many modern playwrights, Claudel tosses Time around like a plaything. The cosmos alone holds the secrets of how Time is to be arranged. Here is a vital facet of modern French theatre. Temporality is no longer to be measured, meted out precisely. It has other types of strengths. Scientific time is perhaps a misnomer. Our human measuring rods are impotent to seize the whole. Sciences, including physics, have no perfect techniques of determining the totality of Time. The Satin Slipper is built on this premise.

Guillaume Apollinaire was a fanciful will o' the wisp. Poet, storyteller, art critic, soldier, lover, traveller, adventurer. He encountered Alfred Jarry at literary meetings sponsored by La Plume, a periodical. Friendly with Picasso, the poet Max Jacob, and the painter, Marie Laurencin, Apollinaire participated in the ebullient art life of his age. He recognized, among the first, the value of cubism, praising Derain, Matisse, Vlaminck and Braque. Apollinaire became interested in theatre. Here, he was an important precursor of surrealism.

In 1903, Apollinaire wrote Les Mamelles de Tiresias (The Breasts of Tiresias), except for the prologue and the last scene of the second act, seven years after Jarry's Ubu the King had first scandalized Paris. Its debut was on June 24, 1917 at the Conservatoire Renée Maubel in Montmartre.

As Bettina Knapp has noted,[13] The Breasts of Tiresias is a valid testimony of a new ars dramatica. Fragmented, rollicking dream, cubistic experiment, it has had considerable influence on music, poetry, drama, and the modern novel since 1917. Apollinaire foresees the avant-garde modern theatre.

At the Conservatoire Maubel, the initial performance of the drama drew very mixed critical reactions. Some called it "crude symbolism"; others blamed its bad taste and vulgarity. A few Cubist painters attacked the play, believing that it was directed against Cubism.

---

[13] Bettina L. Knapp, in (ed., Jacques Guicharnaud) Anthology of 20th Century French Theatre, Les Mamelles de Tiresias (Paris-New York: Paris Book Center, 1967), p. 44.

Those on the favorable side liked its humor and its élan.

Paris, gray and pessimistic, in the early 1900's, required (as Apollinaire thought) transformation by the lively arts. He combined gesture, sound, dancing, poetry, painting, acrobatics, whimsy, dashes of color, imaginative and wild decor, seeking unity of aural and visual spectra.

France needed children. The birthrate had fallen. Apollinaire's spoof concentrates on this social phenomenon as pretext. He imagines willful proliferation of babies. The supposed scene is "Zanzibar." From time to time, this spurious milieu is identified with Paris. Spatial identity is mocked. Zanzibar is triple in meaning: besides the two geographical locales, it was a game of Apollinaire's day in France played with a dice box and two or three dice.

Zanzibar, beyond Time and Space of any usual sort, is really a feeling: gaiety, fancifulness, color, choreography, whimsicality, verve, virility. Time and Space are of little avail.

Apollinaire, he claimed, had invented the adjective surrealist.[14] He consequently wrote, "When man wanted to imitate walking, he created the wheel, which does not resemble a leg. He thus made surrealism without knowing it."[15]

The bizarre, the unimaginable were modes Apollinaire made his own in The Breasts of Tiresias. Seriousness in fancy. The very definition of one kind of poetry.

The subject of his drama, according to Apollinaire, is "so moving in my opinion, that it allows even that one give to the word drama its most tragic sense; but it is up to the French people, if they want to start

---

14 Apollinaire, cited by Bettina L. Knapp, in Ibid., p. 46.
15 Apollinaire, cited by Bettina L. Knapp, in Ibid., p. 46.

13

making children again, for the work to be called, henceforth, a farce."[16]

Mingling of dramatic levels: tragedy, farce, in this unheard-of fantasy, The Breasts of Tiresias. Babies, babies. France was crying out for them. Thérèse, the heroine, is a curious avant-garde embodiment of modern feminism. She wants to be philosopher, soldier, doctor, artist, senator, mathematician. Thérèse spurns her femininity, launching a red and a blue balloon in the air: her breasts. She grows a beard and a moustache. Her husband has no tangible identity. Thérèse changes her name to Tiresias, the blind prophet of Thebes.

Thérèse represents, for one thing, the ability to see into the future. The unwinding of the farce suggests Apollinaire's viewpoint: women, trying to emancipate themselves, lose their place in society.

Miracle births occur in Act II, scene 1. Unaided by women, the husband has brought into the world 40,050 children. In the end, Thérèse returns to her husband to take up again her twin role as wife and mother.

A play, according to Apollinaire, is not an imitation: "For the play must be a complete universe/ With its creator/ That is to say nature itself."[17]

Eminently modern, this statement by Apollinaire is a crux of his dramaturgy. The play is to be a universe, self-contained, not dependent on this world's notions of place or time. Zanzibar is everywhere, or potentially everywhere, the realm of fantasy and sparks, of magic childbirths--40,050 by one person in a day--, of marvelous colors worthy of Cubists.


Jean Cocteau's Orphée (Orpheus), first produced in 1926, transcends Space. It has a hero who shuttles from earth to Hell. He walks through a mirror, sign of

---

16 Apollinaire, cited by Bettina L. Knapp, Ibid., p. 46.
17 Apollinaire, Prologue, Les Mamelles de Tiresias, in op. cit., p. 56.

Death. Heurtebise, a glazier, is suspended in mid-air.
The noise of a time-machine ("on peut employer le 'va-
cuum-cleaner'") denotes how time is being manipulated.
Orpheus' living room "looks pretty much like a magician's
parlor. In spite of the April sky and its direct light,
one imagines this salon surrounded by mysterious forces.
Even familiar objects have a suspicious look."[18]

When familiar objects and time are transformed,
life is radically upset. Cocteau's characters are unreal, highly charged with poetry, dream-bound. "Distortion is the order of this universe,"[19] wrote Oreste
Pucciani in 1954. The statement is profound. Never
before the twentieth century, perhaps, had man felt so
pervasive a malaise screening his understandings. The
twistings of Fate, but even more of the machine age and
its repressive dealings, are proofs that our world is
warped.

Apollinaire, in his frolicking, tongue-in-cheek
style, intimated half-frivolous contortion of the
world's visions. Thérèse misshapes into a pseudo-man.
Her husband gives birth to thousands of children in a
single day.

The data given out by the cosmos have fallen into
disrepute. Hamlet said resoundingly, "The time is out
of joint." In King Lear, Gloucester, has called the
King "O ruined piece of nature." The macrocosm has
shattered man's orderly role in it. He is in shreds.
King Lear and Hamlet are clearly modern in this respect.

Alfred Jarry's universe is topsy-turvy. Evil sup-
plants good. Ubu, the beastly usurper, devours men more
avariciously than fish or fowl. He throws them into his
infamous trappe, a devilish mechanism from which there
can be no escape. Death overtakes Life. This is
distortion in the highest degree.

---

[18] Jean Cocteau, Orphée, in op.cit., (ed. Michèle
Jones), p. 338.

[19] Oreste Pucciani, The French Theater since 1930
(Boston: Ginn, 1954), p. 15.

The cosmos, as reflected by this world, is incoherent and jumbled in "Dada" plays of 1916-1921. Dada was a bizarre overturning in the arts. After 1914 in Zurich, the Dada revolutionaries began to receive publicity. Dada proclaimed its purposes with vehemence. It was belligerently anti-literary. It provoked. At bottom, Dada intended to disrupt the pathways of regularity in the arts, to throw a firebomb into their midst.

Tristan Tzara, poet-dramatist, Hans Arp, painter, and other expatriates in Zurich led the battle. Tzara and his followers averred that they would undermine the theatre's "romantic illusionism" to install their own dramas, raggle-taggle combinations of inventive words and disconnected scenes. Some were inspired in part by artistic collages, mixtures of newspaper clippings, photographs, and paint.

This revolution was not merely silly, as some critics have tried to maintain. Its roots were deep. Dada blasted the idea of the supposed reality of happenings on the stage. In this respect, it was salutary. The theatre of realism gets drab, long-winded, dull. Unreal, Dada arched high, too high. It came close at times to wrecking standard concepts of theatre with its highjinks.

One could have applied derogatory descriptions to Dada plays: gobbledy-gook, inane, futile, hybrid, fantasmagoria, childish. Not so. Dada digs into the subconscious mind's vagaries and wanderings, its freakishness, scattering around pastiches of possible lives. Probably the first important Dada play was staged by Tristan Tzara in 1916: The First Celestial Adventure of M. Antipyrine. Comoedia, a theatre magazine, announced:

> The costumes are surprising, unexpected, ridiculous. They clearly evoke the drawings imagined by madmen and correspond perfectly to the inconceivable text by M. Tristan Tzara.[20]

---

[20] Cited by J. H. Matthews, Theatre in Dada and Surrealism (Syracuse, Syracuse U. Press), 1974, pp. 19-20.

Tzara's text was highly fantastic, broken into bits.

MR. CRICI:   Dsichiloli Mgabati Baïlunda

THE PREGNANT WOMAN:   Toundi-a-voua
                      Soco Bgaï Affahou

MR. BLEUBLEU:         Farafangama Soco Bgaï
                      Affahou[21]

Tzara had earlier outlined what Dada meant to do by
its strange components:

The theater. Since it still remains
attached to a romantic imitation of life, to
an illogical fiction, let us give it all the
natural vigor it had to begin with--let it be
amusement or poetry.[22]

Burlesque tintinnabulation, this pseudo-African
dialect, created by Tristan Tzara, smacks the senses.
He is not simply playing with sound. The poet is
bringing to life new consonances, new rhythms, new
sonorous images, hermetic and nonsensical. Life's tat-
ters of speech, worn away by constant use, open up as
weird vocables replace them.

Bastion of drama, "meaning" collapses. Sequential
clarity falls apart. What binds drama narrowly, veri-
similitude, is thrown to dust. Dada discredits logic
and many approaches to it. Drama and its language
suffer mightily when Dada seeps in. Reason wavers on
the frontiers of disappearance. The reign of reason-
ableness on stage was in peril for those few spectators
who took Dada seriously. A new, highly uncertain cosmos splashes into being.

Sequence in thought, the base of theatre, was replaced by Dada with splintered perspectives, wild, often
incoherent words, collages rather than poster-type
logic, anti-lifelikeness. Time and Space are splintered;
doubt remains.

---

21 Ibid., p. 21.

22 Tristan Tzara, "Guillaume Apollinaire," Dada,
   No. 2, December 1917.

When plot is muddied or destroyed, language tossed around like paper toys, what happens to theatre? What remains? Esoteric results: sound, rhythm, imagery go haywire, build a new universe. Is this any longer a play? Dadaists, and later the surrealists, claimed that this incoherence was de rigueur in a world where traditional values and modes of being were being upset every instant. This is the problem of Dada.

Is disconnectedness enough? Most spectators, at first bemused by Dadaist manifestations, quickly turned away. Dada was a pill too large to swallow. Coherence, after all, was the cornerstone of Western thought, not to be thrown into the winds for the sake of adventure.

Dada bludgeons the brain to sense and think in patterns no one can yet define. This new drama's raisond'etre is to formulate what is unknown. Theatre must, said the Dadaists (who loved theory) drive us away from the ruts of the known. Tzara's First Celestial Adventure of M. Antipyrine abruptly seizes the tail of language:

M. ANTIPYRINE:  Soco Bgaï Affahou
                    Zoumbai zoumbai zoum

M. CRICRI:  il n'y a pas d'humanité il y a
               des réverbères et les chiens
               ("there is no humanity there
               are street lamps and dogs")
               daïn aha dzïn aha bobabo Tyao
               oahiii hi hii hebooum
               ieha ieha

M. BLEUBLEU:  incontestablement[23]
               ("incontestably")

What is the time? Sheer bizarrerie. Where is the space? Somewhere between Africa and France, or a wild fusion of the two.

M. Bleubleu seems to be bedazzled by his interlocutor's rhetoric. Note that Dada here uses repetend (Zoumbai/ zoumbai/ zoum; dzïn/ dzïn/ oahiii hi hii) in a fairly traditional way. Usual syntax is broken.

---

[23] Tzara, op.cit., p. 23.

Dada, therefore, is not a hodge-podge of impossible bits of language. It reverts momentarily, when necessary, to the conceivable. All the same, it spawns a new world: weird, broken into bits, fantasmagoric, seemingly timeless and at certain instants spaceless. Relativity, as Einstein saw it, is here curiously paralleled by social and linguistic relativity. M. Cricri's claim, "Il n'y a pas d'humanité il y a des réverbères et les chiens" effaces human nature. The rest, once the hyperbole is swallowed, is relative to imperfect perceptions. Who is left to perceive? The poet still tries. Physics in Einstein's time had conveyed the imperfections inherent in human measurements.

Dada had a series of implied connections: "daddy," a child's hobby horse, hobby, silly occupation, "bla bla." It was above all a burlesque signal, a rallying cry. Its value, deemed by some critics to be intrinsic, was perhaps greater in its inciting of surrealism, the important artistic revolt of the 1920's and 1930's.

Some Dada poets and playwrights moved into the surrealistic bath. Others came from an allied group ironically named Littérature (1919): André Breton, Philippe Soupault, Louis Aragon, Paul Eluard. Entranced by Paris, many Dadaists and borning surrealists came to the French capital after 1920.

Surrealism in Paris had an outstanding ringleader: André Breton, a psychologist-poet-playwright. He became the editor of a series of ringing surrealist manifestoes, the most important being that of 1924. Freud was a major influence. Breton was enamored of depth psychology. In a historic piece of theoretical work, Breton came out with bold statements: the need to follow psychic automatisms, using transcriptions of dream, or automatic writing when a poet is partly without consciousness.

Such precepts should not be taken as a the whole core of surrealistic theory. Breton, as a postscript, added that control by the reason could in some circumstances be employed by a poet. Many critics fail to take this into cognizance. It is central. Anti-logic, while present, is not the only basis of surreal poetry or drama. This, too, is important. Sheer dream made visible on stage is seldom or never feasible. Unpredictability reigns. But not completely. In this way, the Heisenburg principle of indeterminacy is distantly reflected in dramatic form. No one knows in advance what may happen.

In their dramas, surrealists come to grips with a certain necessity of artistic form. It is sometimes considerable. Semi-orderly dialogue rises up in a few surrealistic plays.

Freudian touches enter in. A childlike state of grace, sought avidly by a number of these dramatists, is nearly impossible to attain. Surrealism seeks to pierce the bone of reason, revealing combinations of conscious and subconscious. A child's fresh faculties of perception are sought after. The images born of such a quest are unworldly, now and then inane. A poet finds a cornerstone of feeling, of expression. At that point the psyche, freed, is uncertain, fragmented, disconnected. It errs, trying out routes of untold expressiveness.

Theory is often belied by practice. Poets deviate from their assertions. They go ahead, as if willy-nilly, damaging theories, bringing back structure and consonance, toward poles of the unknowable. Most found it necessary to recapture elements of form and dialogue which would not have been disavowed, at least in part, by standardized writers. Plots, prime facets of drama, have a wide range: semi-lucidity to incongruity.

What was surrealism? Its claims? Its actual results? Breton's 1924 manifesto elaborated a lengthy set of principles. More intriguing, nevertheless, are the plays themselves. The primary quality of a fine surrealistic poem or play is not its supposed breaking of previous rules on a wholesale scale. Imagery, touchstone of poetry and many kinds of plays, is constructed by a surrealist playwright in new ways. Central images, as well as insignificant ones, may be felt by the reader as unified distantly or less distantly with other images, all of them created from an artist's whimsies, tempered by his good judgment.

Surrealism lives and dies by this fusion. True, many an image is obfuscated or overshadowed by a stronger one. The weak one may fade away. Theory is secondary. What lives on stage (or, on the other hand, is too pale for our memory to retain it) is what counts. The rest of Breton's precepts in his manifestoes were

20

influential more in the breach than in the keeping.

Seven principles dominate Breton's early recipes for surrealism.

1. Liberation of the subconscious (influences: Freud, Rimbaud, etc.)

2. The unregulated and passionate use of the stupefying image.

3. "Submission to dreams, to surprise in them the 'psychic automatism' in all its purity."

4. Recourse to "automatic writing," under the dictation of the subconscious.

5. Absolute rupture of the traditional limits of poetry (form, rhythm, themes, styles, etc.)

6. Liberation of the visionary instinct: images of inhuman worlds, partly animal or vegetal, fantastic: imaginary and unconscious revelations of an unlimited universe, without boundary walls. Violence, cruelty, bizarrerie, incongruities: sardonic or weird humor.

7. Supreme paradox: all this liberation deriving from the unconscious can if necessary be submitted eventually (in the poem) to the control of reason.

Surrealism was itself a paradox. It dictated. Even when poets followed a certain number of these dictates, which was often not the case, the doctrine was arbitrary. Freeing subconscious impulses is at best partial, fragmentary. The control of reason, admitted as a final step by Breton, vitiated some of this freedom, or at least freedom in its totality.

Surrealists flouted time and occasionally, space. But this was not systematic. Dada had paved this path. Einsteinian time, as based on the speed of light and the impossibility of entirely accurate measurements, implies a slight degree of cosmic uncertainty. Similarly, the best surrealist dramatists convey the most uncertain rhythms and lengths of time. Time is radically sapped, by comparison with playwrights of Ibsen's time.

Surrealism filled a gap in French theatrical his-

21

tory. Realism was moribund, except for worn-out formulae in Parisian boulevard playhouses. No strong substitute was apparent.

Tristan Tzara's The Gas Heart (1920), one of the most famous Dada plays, shows transitional aspects leading to surrealism. Metamorphosed beings perform (Mouth, Nose, Eye, Eyebrow). Time, going beyond uncertainty, loses its identity, becoming personified with mustaches:

We have the time, alas, time is lacking
no longer. Time wears mustaches now like
everyone, even women and shaven Americans.
Time is compressed--the eye is weak--but it
isn't yet in the miser's wrinkled purse.[24]

Dada thus eclipsed traditional concepts of time and of the essence of human nature. The device here is elementally metaphorical. All the same, it confers a new status on persons as on time. Time wears a mustache. Its sheer unpredictability (not totally distinct from Heisenburg's theory) is a basis of surrealism, as of Dada. Science and literature, though not identical twins, take on elements of brotherhood.

Dada and negation were as one.

To utter any judgment, to claim to distinguish the true from the false, is a mark of ridiculous presumption, for actually nothing can be contradicted. At about the same time Einstein's theory was encouraging people to believe that everything was relative to circumstance, to men, and that nothing in the world had any importance at all.[25]

Einstein's theory of relativity partly coincided in

24 Tristan Tzara, The Gas Heart, cited in Michael
Benedikt and George Wellwarth, Modern French
Theatre (N.Y.: Dutton, 1966), p. 137.

25 Marcel Raymond, From Baudelaire to Surrealism,
pref. Harold Rosenberg (New York: Wittenborn,
1950), p. 270.

time with Dada and surrealism.  It percolated down.
Without mentioning Einstein by name, Dadaists and surrealists espoused certain lines analogous to his ideas
on relativity in time and space.  To be more accurate,
such theories were webbed in the moment; intellectuals
talked about them, were baffled by them, were affected
by them.

Dada, with its relativistic sparks, excited spectators and participants.  The Gas Heart had its premiere
in Paris with professional actors in 1923.  Paul Eluard,
a representative of Tzara's Dada faction, engaged in
fisticuffs on stage with André Breton.  Breton was the
acknowledged leader of a new literary school on the
horizon, the surrealists.  It was a literary event.

Dada's flourishing, between 1914 and 1921, reflected the general public's disillusionment and dark senti-
ments after World War I.  About 1921, some Dada writers
began to assert that a movement founded on nihilism
ought to consider abolishing itself.  A younger brother,
surrealism, was hovering in the wings, ready to supplant
it.

Surrealism, the coming trend, had different sources.
André Breton's private preoccupations, his interest in
psychiatry mainly, were the predominant forces in play
during the first years of surrealism.  Many Paris Dadaists joined Breton's group of surrealists after 1921.
Louis Aragon's The Clothes Closet One Fine Evening
(1922) exemplifies early surrealism on stage.  Lenore
and Jules, husband and wife, are the leading characters.
The sparse intrigue centers around a clothes closet,
into which Lenore forbids Jules to penetrate.  It is a
mystery, surreal fashion.  She threatens him:

If you open it, then the sun and the
stars will be extinguished, the rain will
enter my bones and into your eyes of coal.[26]

Aragon, like his fellow surrealists, twists the

---

[26] Louis Aragon, The Clothes Closet One Fine
Evening, cited in Robert G. Marshall and Frede-
ric C. St. Aubyn, Trois pièces surréalistes
(New York: Appleton-Century Crofts, 1969), p. 60.

idea of the universe to his own purposes. Sun and stars will go out, losing their heat and light, says Lenore, if Jules opens the clothes closet. The individual affects cosmic order. Fantastic metaphor, Lenore's exclamation shapes the surrealists' tendency to see the cosmos as a function of man.

Space slides away. This, too, is found in some other surrealist plays. Einstein's implied measurements of time, involving the speed of light and opening the way to the nuclear bomb, come to literary usage here, not directly but in a refracted sense. Lenore foresees the possibility of sun and stars losing their current potency because of what human beings do.

Near the end of the play, Jules lyrically broadcasts:

> And the sun which is never again going
> to set nor rise, but which will henceforth
> run like a madman on the roads and in the
> beds of women without modesty, laughing,
> rohahihi, laughing.[27]

The sun, a primary image, is again controlled by man. Why should a surrealist poet like Aragon have decided to choose the sun as an extravagant facet of human existence? Surrealism liked the violent, often the burning force capable of transforming everything in its way. Jules changes the sun into a near-human being with potentialities of leaping into the beds of immodest women.

In Roger Vitrac's Victor or Children to Power (1924), one of surrealism's masterpieces, the boy-hero revolts against his family and putrid middle-class society. He courts Lili:

> You will stay. You will stay, my
> dear Lili. Image of heaven. Cat's head-
> gear. Stalk of moons, you will stay.[28]

---

27 Ibid., p. 70.
28 Roger Vitrac, Victor ou les enfants au pouvoir, in Ibid., Acte I, p. 87.

24

The imagery of moons and heaven, in itself, would not go far. Victor, who incarnates the role of a boyish, surrealist poet, sees moonstalks and heaven in Lili as spontaneously as though he were assigning her qualities of lakes and meadows. This is what is important. Vitrac, as author, participates metaphorically with the moon and heaven. It is active juncture, not mere poetizing. Lili is moon substance; she is heaven. Once more, space and time fritter away from their usual boundaries. The epoch of Einstein has left its mark in metaphors and paradoxes such as those of Victor or Children to Power.

In If You Please, (1920), by André Breton and Philippe Soupault, Paul and Valentine are talking. Paul explains, "You have to keep a certain distance from the house to rouse an echo. With all those we love our hope is to be able to embrace the trunk of this supraterrestrial tree."29

Supraterrestrial, a strange adjective in this context, springs to view. A tree growing in space, as it were. Breton and Soupault use a characteristic surrealist device. Images of earth and outer space merge. This union of two incongruous and distant ideas is basic. It constitutes much of the strength of surrealist poetics.

Later Valentine says, "It's the beginning of paradise, or so it seems. The gray, slaty day has blue automobile horns; at night one flies on a silvery frond."30

What is paradise? Valentines, differing from Hollywood pictures of paradise on earth, changes elements of living. The slaty day is given car horns; by night everyone flies over a silvery frond. Space, again, is transformed by the surrealist. That is to say, he jumbles concepts of space so that the reader envisions an entirely different world. This is surrealism's captious tour de force.

---

29 Benedikt and Wellwarth, op. cit., p. 149.

30 Ibid., p. 150.

The Mysteries of Love (1924), by Roger Vitrac, is
an unsuccessful attempt to transpose human and animal
essences in a love story. Its stage setting is extraordinary:

> The stage simultaneously represents a
> railway station, a dining car, the seashore,
> a hotel lobby, a yard-goods shop, the main
> square of a provincial town.[31]

Simultaneity of setting, often effective, is not a
new technique. But the dizzying multiplicity of Vitrac's
decor (6 scenes) is unusual. Why? The playwright
apparently wanted not to use the technique of separating
six scenes so as to suggest that in art, large numbers
of events can be encountered at one time.

The universe itself is dynamic. Einstein, with
Alexander Friedmann, predicted this. Few of us take
this to heart. Our ingrained customs of thought and
action have assumed for centuries that the outside
world is, in the end, static, definable. Here is an
upsetting concept. It is also vital. The energies of
an atom, with the nuclear bomb, are Titans hanging over
us at every instant.

Surrealist plays, with all their extravaganzas and
excesses, their bombast and splinterings, were in tune
with this prediction. A dynamo rules in their wildest
dramas. Some force beyond visible control pushes everything into a chaotic state. The cosmos rushes ahead,
inexorable, kinetic, ever-changing. Surrealism, more
highly charged with these energies than realism, im-
pressionism, and standard forms of French theatre since
1896, thus reflected in some ways an important part of
Einsteinian physics.

As Lincoln Barnett pointed out,[32] space and time
are really intuition. There is no objective reality in
space except for the way the objects we perceive are
ordered or arranged. Events, by their order, make us
perceive time, which has no independent existence.

---

31 Ibid., p. 253.

32 Lincoln Barnett, The Universe and Dr. Einstein
(New York: Bantam, 1974), p. 19.

Surrealism, by breaking time into bits and crumbling its consistency, brought something radically new into French theatre. Henceforth, spectators could no longer hope to see real-life figures always engaged in real-life problems on stage, in semblances of measureable time spans. Likewise, spatial norms were beginning to be crushed; a viewer might find himself confronted with six different locales simultaneously. Once more, drama and physics share bedcovers. Not partners, the two show marked affinities, unnoticed by all but a very few critics. The similarity is natural: the great thoughts of those days came from Marx, Freud, and Einstein.

27

# CHAPTER III

No phenomenon could be a phenomenon until it was an observed phenomenon, asserted Einstein. What does this mean? Nothing is an event until it is observed. This gives to the role of the observer a highly prejudicial standpoint. Is such a precept applicable to drama? Of course it is. About 1830, Alfred de Musset, the French poet-playwright, was writing short plays for what he called "Un Spectacle dans un Fauteuil." Supposedly, they were designed for reading in an armchair. Most were eventually performed. What is interesting is the pretext. Musset thought that a drama could be artistically taken in without performance. Today his unplayed drama, La Coupe et les livres, is practially forgotten. It could never be classed as a lasting event.

In French dramatic literature since 1896, there are innumerable examples of plays performed. This is well known. What if a friend reads our play, sitting in a comfortable armchair, with a glass of cognac? Is this a phenomenon, an event? The observer's definition counts. If the play is strikingly or passably beautiful, and he remembers the occasion, it is certainly an event for him. Is one observer enough? Yes, I would say. A witness has been present. A phenomenon has taken place. Scientifically, this is difficult to measure. Humanly, the measurement is clear-cut.

Einstein was not only a physicist of genius. When he had become famous, in his later years, he espoused two great norms for human behavior: the abolition of war and an end to hatred of Jews. He was a leading Zionist.

The knowledge of science is conducive to faithful championing of social causes. This was not only true of Einstein; many scientists join in appeals for aid to starving countries or to political causes.

If this is true, why should we be astonished that some of the greatest scientific discoveries by men like Einstein are reflected, more or less directly, in all sorts of human affairs, including the theatre?

Fernando Arrabal, born in 1933 in Melilla, Spanish Morocco, who has made his home in Paris since 1954, is one of the most fantasmagoric playwrights alive. As a boy, he suffered the agonies of Franco's Spain. His father disappeared. There are intimations in Arrabal's work that he may have suspected his mother of having denounced his father to the police. A terrific split in his personality attests to his early upbringing and to this tragic death, for which he has never forgiven the authorities in Spain. Bizarrerie and cruelty are his hallmarks. Arrabal is not comparable to any other living dramatist. Categories--surrealist, for instance --do not fit. There is ruthlessness of purpose and method in his plays.

Arrabal, who despised military authoritarianism and war itself, wrote tellingly of these convictions in his first novel, Baal Babylone. He became an anti-militarist. Guernica (inspired by Picasso's famous painting) and most of all Picnic on the Battlefield (1959) beat hard at the same theme.

Picnic on the Battlefield[1] is a small masterpiece. It reeks with burlesque, with the hatred of an obsessed poet for war. It is mythic. Spurious soldier on a dream battlefield, Zapo is a memorable figure. At the antipodes are his parents, sticky bourgeois, who decide to visit him and to picnic on the battlefield where he is engaged in warfare. The fantasy is ironic. Its conclusion: neither juvenile candor and its simiplicity nor the self-satisfaction which rivets the bourgeois parents to beliefs coming from another epoque are any longer sufficient. A very different menace, fatalistic, confronts them.

An enemy soldier, Zepo, appears. Zepo is in green, Zapo in gray. The parents are playing a pasodoble, a characteristic Spanish dance tune, on a phonograph. Zepo is entranced. Zapo discovers Zepo, helf-hidden. Both hold up their hands. The parents, M. et Mme Tepan, coerce Zapo into tying up his prisoner. Suddenly Zapo asks his father and mother to take a photograph of him standing on Zepo's belly. The ludicrous overwhelms the warlike.

---

[1] Fernando Arrabal, Pique-nique en campagne, in Panorama du théâtre nouveau, vol. 3, Le Théâtre de la Dérision (eds. Jacques G. Bonay and Reinhard Kuhn), (New York: Appleton-Century Crofts, 1967).

Arrabal was imbued with a hatred of and derision for
war. Can it be abolished? This farfetched aspiration,
also held by Einstein, a brilliant scientist, pierces
his drama. Zepo protests at the inglorious picture of
himself beneath Zapo's foot. One day, he says, his fiancée will see the picture and claim that he is inca-
pable of making war properly.

M. Tepan enjoins Zapo, "Look like a hero." Deri-
siveness, in an unlikely civilian-ordained situation on
a battlefield, is high in color. Nowhere in any authen-
tic war have embattled soldiers acted like this. Is
this pasodoble dance or machine-gun fire? This is the
play's suspense.

Zapo now invites Zepo to share a luncheon along
with M. et Mme Tepan, who have brought a bonne bouteille.
The Tepans exult; they assert that they have passed an
excellent day à la campagne. (A play on words, since in
French campagne means either campaign or countryside.)

Bombers fly over. Their bombshells fall very near
the stage. Deafening roars. Mme Tepan, very calm, goes
to find an umbrella. Like rain, or so it seems. Her
husband holds out a hand from beneath the umbrella to
test the atmosphere. All clear. Zapo and Zepo have
taken cover. Warily, they come out. M. Tepan, almost
laughing, says, "Oh, little bombs like these. What a
laugh!"[2]

Two Red Cross men arrive, carrying a stretcher.
"No dead around here?" they ask. And they are disap-
pointed when Zapo assures them that no one has been
killed. "What a mess we're in!" they exclaim. "Not
even wounded? What a lousy trick!" M. Tepan, angry,
scolds Zapo and Zepo: "You might as well say right
away that you don't want to do a single thing to help
these gentlemen, who are so gracious!" The first Red
Cross stretcher-bearer says, "All we can do is hope
that we'll be luckier in a trench, that they'll all be
dead."[3]

Irony at its most derisive. Mock battle, mock

---

2 Ibid., p. 30.
3 Ibid., p. 31.

31

heroics, mock eagerness to find dead on the part of Red Cross men, all is mockery. Arrabal's play is sheer raillery. War is gentlemanly posing, intellectual shambles. Death on the battlefield is mathematics, counting up of bodies for someone's scorecard. War, supreme agony of mankind, is spoofed with great sardonic effect.

Zepo, called to war, had been told by his father that he couldn't go because he had no horse. He asked the recruiter if he could take his fiancée along. No. Then what about my aunt, asked Zepo, for every Thursday she makes cream for me. I really like that.

When soldiers get bored during a war, suggests M. Tepan, there is a simple answer. Stop war. And everybody goes home. Terrific, answers Zapo.[4]

Again, Mme Tepan begins to play a record. Again, a pasodoble. A military telephone rings. No one hears it. Zapo dances with Zepo and Mme Tepan dances with her husband. Unheeding the telephone, they continue to dance. Once again, the telephone. On goes the dance. With a tremendous fracas, bombs, firearm spurts, and machine-gun fire break out. Having realized not a single thing, the four continue their joyous pasodoble. All at once, a storm of machine-gun fire mows the four down together. They fall to the ground, stiff and dead. Naturally, the phonograph goes on playing the same pasodoble tune, time after time. The phonograph has been damaged. Naturally, in come the two Red Cross stretcher-bearers in search of the dead, their litter empty. Curtain.

War is a pasodoble. Arrabal reduces warfaring tragedy to a perpetually-repeating rengaine. Picnic on the Battlefield masterfully flattens the very idea of war. Childish games, childish notions, fiancées and horses, dances and joy take the place of deadly combat. Zapo and Zepo the Tepans are ours. They shine through us, through our terror of war, our intellectual realization that systematic killing of enemies is futile. Picnic on the Battlefield is a comically wry stance. Arrabal despises every form of bellicosity. The play guides us toward sense, toward peace.

---

4 Ibid., p. 36.

Twenty-six years earlier, the French dramatist Jean Giraudoux had produced La Guerre de Troie n'aura pas lieu (Tiger at the Gates) (1935),5 a sort of paradoxical counterpoint to Arrabal's Picnic on the Battlefield (1961). Giarudoux, a diplomat, had witnessed first hand the maneuverings of both France and Germany prior to World War II. He had fought valiantly in the first World War. He suffered wounds. Awarded the honor of Chevalier de la Légion d'Honneur because of his war record, Giraudoux was the first French writer to win this distinction.

Lover of Greek letters and of his native province in France, Le Limousin, (near the inland city of Limoges), Giraudoux had a double attitude toward war. This ambivalence haunts Tiger at the Gates. Giraudoux had seen battlefield heroes; he was one himself. On the other hand, he found the very idea of slaughter odious.

Some critics have tried to term Tiger at the Gates pacifistic. This is true only in small part. The whole play exudes inevitability. War is coming, as the Trojan War was coming. Inexorably, battle is to begin. Giraudoux was not a pacifist. His sober drama, echoing the Greek tragedy, the Trojan War, is a fight predestined to lose. There is no recourse.

In the first scene, Andromaque, who wants only peace, asks Cassandre "Why should the war take place? Paris doesn't want Helen any longer. Helen doesn't want Paris any longer."6

Cassandre, mockingly, retorts, "Have you ever seen Destiny interested in negative phrases?"7 Cassandre represents the voice of fatality, pessimistic to the core. She knows that war is coming and lets the others hear this gloominess.

---

5 Jean Giraudoux, La Guerre de Troie n'aura pas lieu (ed. Maurice Mercier) (Paris: Classiques Larousse, 1959).

6 Ibid., p. 28.

7 Ibid., p. 28.

Hector returns, embraces Andromaque. Cassandre lurks in the offing to say something to Hector. The returning hero wonders, "Do you have something to say to me?" speaking to Cassandre. Andromaque interjects, "Don't listen to her!...Some catastrophe!" Hector, "Speak!" Cassandre, "Your wife is bearing a child." This revelation intensifies Hector's central problem: how to bring peace to Troy.

"My son will not be a coward, says Andromaque. But I will have cut off the index finger of his right hand." Hector, in one of the most ironic speeches in the play, retorts, "If every mother cuts off the index finger of her son, the armies of the universe will fight wars without index fingers."[8] Hector is a veteran of war and sardonically foresees more wars in the future.

Despite the valiant efforts of Hector and Ulysses, his antagonist, the Trojan gates open at the end of Tiger at the Gates and war is presaged. In the gates, Helen is embracing Troilus, youngest son of Priam and Hecubus. One of the deepest of all the play's ironies, the highly-charged, erotic Helen is promoting war by her lascivious conduct. The Trojan war will take place. War will take place.

Fernando Arrabal's Picnic on the Battlefield, denunciation of the barbarism of war and its inanities, is an indirect dramatic analogy of Einstein's untiring striving for peace. Of course, a playwright uses very different materials in his battle for peace. Arrabal is a wild, unbridled poet in the theatre. His imagery is at times child-like, at times morbidly mature. What really matters, however, is not so much the means employed by Einstein and a young dramatist. Their purposes (shocking the public into a realization that war is a dreadful monster) are not unlike each other, basically.

Giraudoux, on the other hand, while seeming to say that war is inevitable, is really pleading for sense and balance in dealings among modern nations. A great dialogue between Hector and Ulysses, justly famous, embodies this yearning.

---

[8] Ibid., pp. 30-31.

The destiny of our planet, studied today with extraordinarily scrupulous care by astronomers and astrophysicists, among others, was foreshadowed in Einstein's special and general theories of relativity. The great physicist opened up innumerable new vistas for those who followed.

John Wheeler asserted that "the greatest crisis in physics of all time"[9] is inherent in Black Holes. "Astronomers now believe that they have discovered at least one black hole, orbiting a giant blue star in the constellation Cygnus some 8,000 light years from earth. Good evidence exists for several more elsewhere."[10]

Einstein's theories, recognized as having been prime forerunners for much in modern astrophysics, have liberated scientific thought on the spheres. Black holes are now part of our imaginative folklore, our movies, our expectations for the future.

It is possible to locate in Einsteinian thought some intriguing concepts which theatre has formulated, not necessarily through physics directly, but on its own. Einstein, in addition to being a physicist, promulgated theories about human behavior. An important chain of ideas, for example, is this:

An individual sees in retrospect a uniformly systematic development, whereas the actual experience takes place in kaleidoscopic particular situations.
The great variety of the external situations and the narrowness of the momentary content of consciousness bring about a sort of atomizing of the life of every human being."[11]

---

[9] John Wheeler, cited in John L. Wilhelm, "A Singular Man," Quest, April 1979, p. 33.

[10] Ibid., p. 33.

[11] Albert Einstein, Autobiographical Notes, ed. Paul Arthur Schilpp (Chicago: Open Court, 1979).

The word atomizing is fascinating. Einstein seemingly wants to apply the term in the meanings implied by physics. In literature and in literary criticism, atomizing is used in a non-scientific sense. Breaking up into the smallest bits, in a simple definition, is the literary way of looking at the word. Einstein, thinking of atoms and their behavior, must have transferred this way of thought into more ordinary human signification.

We see ourselves as having developed in a somewhat straight line, day after day. In truth, a long series of individual situations, each unlike the preceding one, determines us. Like a kaleidoscope. The image is apt. We see variegated colors and shapes in a real kaleidoscope, forever changing. Einstein's view is exact. At any moment in consciousness, we see only that moment. This narrows our inherent vision of the whole range of sensation and time around us.

What is the consequence of Einstein's pronouncement? If we atomize, if we splinter our life into fragments, there are a multitude of outside influences we cannot recognize. We limit ourselves to the immediate. Time, again, is the bête noire. We need to shatter time's hold, to gain further perspectives, beyond the here and now.

On motion, Einstein is peerless. If we want to have entire description of motion, he says, we must specify how the body alters its position with time; i.e., for every point in the trajectory it must be stated at what time the body is situated there.

Among Einstein's conclusions were these:

(1) Nothing could ever exceed the speed of light.

(2) That a metre stick moving at a speed approaching that of light would become shorter and shorter.

(3) That a clock moving likewise would slow and stop if it moved with the speed of light.

(4) That the mass of an object measured by its inertia would become infinitely large in the limit as it reached the speed of light.

These primary formulations of Einstein's, which set

36

the world of physics to buzzing, have few if any literal configurations in modern French drama. It may be that playwrights and poets of the theatre have had extreme difficulty in comrehending such esoteric ideas. On stage, motion is fairly traditional. There are of course exceptions. Jean-Louis Barrault, the French actor, in A Stroll in the Air (1965), by Ionesco, floated in the air for the exigencies of the play. Lack of motion, in Beckett's dramas, is exemplified by Oh les beaux jours (Happy Days, 1963), when Winnie, the heroine, is buried up to the neck but keeps on talking.

Vertiginous growth, incorporated in a huge corpse hidden in a room, suddenly, time after time, taking on several more centimeters, is the theme of Amédée ou comment s'en debarrasser (Amédée or How to Get Rid of It). Husband and wife, Amédée and Madeleine, are confronted with the nearly insuperable task of getting rid of an ever-growing corpse, which threatens their space and their peace of mind.

Nightmarish in its atmosphere of harassment (the entire play, with few exceptions, is Amédée's lack of will power, his refusal to get rid of the corpse somehow), Amédée contains powerful instants.

At the Théâtre de Babylone in Paris, the body was eighteen meters in length; its pants were eight meters long.12 Near the end of the play, with the corpse invading the rest of the apartment, onward, onward, always onward, Amédée resolves to deploy it somewhere else. He and Madeleine drag it through a window, after it has shattered glass and walls.

Curiously, Amédée is twisted around the corpse. This grotesque body has unimaginably taken the shape of an enormous parachute. Amédée takes off into the air. Not simply a director's or author's sleight-of-hand imagination, this trick occasioned, at the Théâtre de Babylone, a mystifying vision of the entire decor rising high above the stage. Quite unexpectedly, the play's ultimate suggestivity is that of a celebration. Life has temporarily overcome death. Ionesco himself, hav-

---

12 Simone Benmussa, Ionesco (Paris: Seghers, 1966), p. 98

ing witnessed a Parisian performance, invoked the twin
terms, grâce et Salut.[13]


In a different system, Einstein had pointed out
that the mass of an object measured by its inertia
would become infinitely large in the limit as it
reached the speed of light. Amédée's struggles with a
corpse that would not cease growing hints, on a comico-
tragic level, that mass is uncontrollable once it begins to take on dizzying speed of growth. Amédée or How
to Get Rid of It, a strange, foreboding, grotesque
comedy, tells the spectator hyperbolically that modern
growth (e.g., world population, crime, complexity of
business operations and international diplomacy) is
dangerous. These warnings, of course, are done by metaphor. The play, by shutting off Amédée's and Madeleine's
vital space, figuratively indicates that world space is
ominously decreasing, to the point where life itself is
in question.

Philosophically, space and time are near-brothers.
On occasion, they are almost like non-identical twins.
Einstein revised Newton's concept that time is absolute,
that it is universally the same, and that it flows
steadily from the past toward the future.[14]

Innumerable modern playwrights in France have toyed
with temporal leaps in their plays. Time, in fact,
conveyed helter-skelter or in an orderly but up-to-date
way, is a staple of modern French theatre. Flashbacks
are monnaie courante. Mingling of past, present, and
future is also frequent. Timelessness is more rare,
but it exists.

Movement is intrinsically related to time and
space. When a French play evokes strange sorts of motions, as Ionesco's Amédée or How to Get Rid of It does,
time is inherent, if not in evidence. Likewise space,
although it may be more obvious in its manifestations.
The three phenomena on stage should be observed together, in so far as possible.

---

13 Ibid., p. 100.

14 "The Year of Doctor Einstein," Time, Feb. 19,
1979, p. 73.

The time/space/movement triangle fills Le Roi se meurt (Exit the King, 1963),[15] by Eugène Ionesco. King Bérenger realizes that he is gradually dying. His two wives, Marguerite, and Marie, look at his impending doom quite differently. Marie has Bérenger's heart. She embodies joie de vivre. Marguerite keeps warning him that death, at last, is really approaching. Time is of the essence. King Bérenger has reigned an indefinite period, over many, many years, perhaps several hundred years. But past time is marvelously eclipsed. Bérenger would like to ignore it. Deeds of other times are carried into the present. The kingdom is slowly rotting. Marguerite says, "the kingdom is full of holes like an immense Gruyère cheese." Marie replies,

"We couldn't do a thing against fatality, against natural erosions." "Not to mention all those disastrous wars," answers Marguerite. "While his drunken soldiers were asleep, at night or after the copious meals at their barracks, neighbors altered in their favor the boundary lines of the King's frontiers. The national territory shrank. His soldiers didn't want to fight."[16]

Space shrinks. The King's proceedings, in turn, have to be shrunken. His movements are constricted. His time on earth, because of the dilapidated status of his kingdom and his unsuccessful wars, is abbreviated. Paradox. He has lived hundreds of years. In addition, Marie and Marguerite, like the King's other subjects, are afraid of limitations on their movements. Marie had the custom of going with the King on honeymoons every three months. Finie la partie. No longer.

"There is a fissure in the wall," remarks a guard.[17] This becomes a symbolic fissure. The King's territories are falling apart. A small spatial dent calls into being the death of a once-powerful kingdom.

---

15 Eugène Ionesco, Le Roi se meurt, in L'Avant-garde théâtrale (ed., Tom Bishop) (Lexington, Mass.: Heath, 1970).

16 Ibid., p. 94.

17 Ibid., p. 90.

Concurrently, Marie and Marguerite are absorbed in the problem of time and the King's health:

"Take all your time," says Marie. "He might have a heart attack." Marguerite answers, "We don't have the time to take our time. Frolicking is over, leisures are over, beautiful days are over, banquet blowouts are over, your strip-tease is over."[18]

What is temporal affects the most intimate feelings of secondary characters like Marie and Marguerite, as well as those of the King himself. Barefooted, the King enters. "I slept badly, this earth which is cracking, these frontiers which are withdrawing...there is really too much noise."[19] Cracks have fissured the King's spatial dominion. Marguerite announces to him, "You are going to die in an hour and twenty-five minutes." His doctor assents. Marie, the fighter, begs, "Don't give up." The King is seated on his throne, Marie by his side.

THE KING: Have time turn back on its steps.
MARIE: Have us be as we were twenty years ago.
THE KING: Have us be last week.
MARIE: Have us be yesterday evening. Time turn back, time turn back; time, stop.
MARGUERITE: There is no more time. Time has melted in his hand.[20]

On the brink of death, the King implores time to return to the past in his footsteps. Marie joins him, enjoining time to be as it was twenty years ago, or even more recently, yesterday evening. Time and space have actually melted together in their wishes, reality of a second.

THE KING: I don't want to die.
MARIE: Alas! His hair has turned white all of a sudden...Wrinkles are accumulating on his brow, on his face. Unexpectedly, he has aged fourteen centuries.
THE DOCTOR: Out of fashion so fast.[21]

---

[18] Ibid., p. 93.
[19] Ibid., p. 96.
[20] Ibid., p. 105.
[21] Ibid., p. 106.

As Einstein has told us, perspectives on time's rapidity or slowness depend on the observer himself. Time is relative to the witness of events. Marguerite here intimates the passage of hundreds of years in the wink of an eyelash. This acceleration, due entirely to her private emotions, is very nearly Einsteinian. Literature again approaches physics.

Marguerite: At forty, you proposed to wait until you were fifty. At fifty...

The King: I was full of life, how full I was of life!

Marguerite: At fifty, you wanted to wait to sixty. You were sixty, ninety, one hundred and twenty-five, two hundred, four hundred years old. You didn't only adjourn your preparations for ten years, but for fifty. Then, you put that off from century to century.

The King: What I had was precisely the intention to begin. Ah! If I could have a century ahead of me, perhaps I would have the time!

The Doctor: You have only one hour left, Sire. You must do everything in one hour.

Marie: He will not have the time, it's not possible. You must give him time.

Marguerite: That is what is impossible. But in one hour, he has all his time.

The Doctor: A well-filled hour is better than centuries of forgetfulness and negligence. Five minutes are enough, ten conscious seconds. He is being given one hour: sixty minutes, three thousand six hundred seconds. He is lucky.

Marguerite: He loafed along the way.

Marie: We reigned, he has worked.

The Guard: Labors of Hercules.

Marguerite:  Puttering around.[22]

Time is a kaleidoscope.  Or it can be collapsed, or
nearly collapsed, by the vision of each person speaking.
In each case, temporal understanding is different.  Only
Marie and the guard have similar insights.  Centuries
can become a few seconds, life becoming death.

Exit the King, one of the beautiful plays of modern
French theatre, approaches its climax.

> The King:   ... Is that beginning?  No.  Why
> was I born if it wasn't forever?  Cursed
> parents.  What a strange idea, what a great
> joke!  I came into the world five minutes
> ago, I was married three minutes ago.
>
> Marguerite:  It has been two hundred and
> eighty-three years.
>
> The King:  I mounted on the throne two and
> a half minutes ago.
>
> Marguerite:  Two hundred seventy-seven years
> and three months ago.
>
> The King:  Not even the time to say Ouch!
> I didn't have time to know life.
>
> Marguerite, to the Doctor:  He didn't make
> a single effort to do that.
>
> Marie:  It was only a brief promenade in a
> flowering lane, an unkept promise, a smile
> which closed upon itself.
>
> Marguerite, to the Doctor, continuing:  All
> the same, he had the greatest learned men to
> explain to him.  And theologians, and experi-
> enced persons, and books that he never read.
>
> The King:  I didn't have the time.
>
> Marguerite, to the King:  You used to say
> that you had all your time.

---

22 Ibid., p. 107.

The King:  I didn't have the time, I didn't
have the time, I didn't have the time.[23]


The King wants to be remembered until the end of
time:  "If they remember me, it will be for how long?
Have them remember until the end of time.  And after
the end of time, in twenty thousand years, in two hundred fifty-five billion years... What must be finished
is already finished."[24]

Eclipsed time dominates this key play by Ionesco.
More unusual, the King looks ahead to the end of the
Cosmos, some two hundred fifty-five billion years hence.
Modern prognosticators, chiefly astrophysicists and physicists, claim that the universe will come to an end,
very likely with a Big Bang, in billions of years.
Whether voluntary or not, the King's forecast that the
world will finish two hundred fifty-five billion years
hence is a curious parallel to present-day scientists'
figures.  A playwright, in speculative irony, comes
somewhat close to scientific insights of how the cosmos
may end.

In Arthur Adamov's La Parodie (The Parody, 1950),
time is one of the ultimate, monstrous absurdities.  As
René Lalou has written, "Adamov..persists in depicting,
with a shuddering sensitivity, in despair, the drama
of our time, lived on the level of pitiful witnesses,
unconscious actors of History on the march."[25]

Leonard Pronko, an astute critic of Anouilh, di-
vides the French author's plays into several groups.  In
the earliest group are the "Black Plays," L'Hermine (The
Ermine), Jezabel, La Sauvage (Restless Heart), Y avait
un prisonnier (Once was a Prisoner), Le voyageur sans
bagage (Traveller without Luggage, 1937), and the "Pink
Plays," Le bal des voleurs (Thieves' Carnival), Le ren-
dez-vous de Senlis (Dinner with the Family), and Léo-
cadia (Time Remembered).

---

23 Ibid., p. 111-112.
24 Ibid., p. 114-115.
25 René Lalou, Le Théâtre en France depuis 1900 (Paris: Presses Universitaires de France, 1961), p.
   121.

The two masterpieces are probably Traveller without Luggage and Thieves' Carnival. Amnesia, in Traveller,[26] is the prime motif. It permits the hero, Gaston, to forget misdeeds from the past. He has obliterated time. But time catches up with him. A succession of ladies looking for lost sons interview him to see if he is indeed their own. The past is now conceivably in the present. And Gaston's future, which he willfully deliberates, will be decided only when he accepts a family of the sort he deems right for him as he now is.

Anouilh's dramatic wellspring can be criticized. Gaston's amnesia as a result of World War I is too facile a pretext for a metaphor of freedom. What has been will be, to a large degree. Gaston had seduced his brother's wife, as well as maids, and has caused a lifetime injury to his best friend. He tries to banish these vicious events from his present existence.

But the Renaud family, which had come to find him, brought time with them, waves of time which Gaston could not fully escape. His former mistress, his brother's wife, identifies him "positively" by a scar on his body. Gaston turns his back on her and on the family. His temporal fate, he believes, lies in future events, not in his sordid past.

Accompanied by triumphant music, Gaston finds a new life: a Little Boy, who is actually Uncle Madensale, has come from England in search of a lost nephew. Gaston, having rejected the Renauds, his real family, is free to leap in whatever direction his spirit tells him to. He finds the Little Boy appealing. When Mr. Truggle, solicitor for the Madensale family, says that his client's nephew has a very slight scar below the left shoulder blade. Gaston pulls off his shirt to reveal his scar, a coincidental facsimile. Gaston accepts the Madensales as "his family." The ending is a bit of trickery. Anouilh is not pulling the wool over our eyes. And the drama does not all of a sudden become intrinsically optimistic. (Anouilh classed it with his "Black Plays.")

Gaston incarnates a curious shape of time. It is different from telescoping. Acts which have taken place

---

26 Jean Anouilh, Le Voyageur sans bagage (Paris: Livre de Poche, 1958).

before the play begins, his misdeeds and mistreatment of
a friend, are wiped clean by the power of Gaston's de-
cision that the sordidness of what his life had been can
be disregarded completely. So the perverse hero has
played with time, juggled it like a toy balloon.

In Traveller without Luggage, unlike in the data of
Einstein's relativity of time, Gaston purportedly
smashes what is temporal in his past, in near-absolutist
fashion. Nothing is left, or so he claims.

Anouilh has audaciously invented a situation where
even scientific concepts of time are obliterated. The
play is a tour de force. We do not believe in Gaston's
future destiny; he cannot rightfully escape the chains
of what is behind him. Traveller without Luggage,
despite defects, is an important modern French play as
it manipulates time, setting it in a new and memorable
guise.

## CHAPTER IV

"I do not believe that civilization will be wiped out in a war fought with the atomic bomb. Perhaps two-thirds of the people of the earth might be killed,"[1] said Albert Einstein.

As a boy, Einstein was dyslexic, late to speak, and scarcely ready to get along within the German school system. His teachers prognosticated that he would amount to nothing. The amazing fact is that within a decade, he went from high school drop-out to formulator of the theory of relativity.

In 1945, Einstein learned of the devastating atomic damage done in Japan to Hiroshima and Nagasaki. Although he had urged President Roosevelt to start work on the atomic bomb, he had no direct part in the technical stages of the nuclear bomb. Scientists, however, knew that his theory of relativity and other ideas had led to the splitting of the atom, and to the bomb itself. A once-dyslexic boy, now a grown physicist, through one of the miracles of modern knowledge, had prepared the way for the most awesome weapons of modern times.

Einstein and fellow scientists launched a vast wave of discovery, especially in physics, which has present-day repercussions. In the last eighty years, man has gained more knowledge of the atomic universe than in all previous human history.

Exact measurements are highly significant in physics. Einstein's pronouncements in his theory of general relativity differed from the mechanics of Newton, and in particular Einstein's predictions, with respect to small-scale phenomena.

"The predictions of general relativity only differ from Newton's theory in smaller amounts and most tests of the theory have been carried out through observations in astronomy."

---

[1] Atlantic Monthly, November, 1945 and November, 1947. As told to Raymond Swing.

For example, Einstein's theory explains
the shift in the perihelion of Mercury, the
bending of light rays in the presence of
large bodies, and the Einstein shift.
The Einstein shift...is a gravitational
red shift. A slight red shift in the lines
of a stellar spectrum due to the gravitational
field of a large body.
...A red shift...is a shift in the spec-
tral lines of many extragalactic stellar spectra towards the red end of the visible spectrum relative to the wave length of these lines
in the terrestrial spectrum. It is thought to
be due to the Döppler effect caused by the
recession of stars...A significant red shift
has recently been determined for a radio
galaxy, implying a very great recessional
velocity."[2]

In Newton's theory of gravitation the
fact that two bodies travel in curved paths
in each other's presence is interpreted as
being due to an interaction between them.
The General Theory of Relativity replaces
this interpretation by the idea that it is
due to the geometric properties of space
itself.

Many attempts have been made to formulate a unified field theory in which the
nuclear and electromagnetic properties also
result from the geometric properties of
spacetime. So far such attempts have been
unsuccessful.[3]

Einstein himself spent a large part of his later
career in exploring the possibilities which might form
a unified field theory. It was an overwhelming enter-
prise, one which he was fated never to conquer.

The unattainable=beauty. "The most
beautiful thing we can experience is the

---

[2] Valerie H. Pitt, ed., The Penguin Dictionary of
Physics (Harmondsworth: Penguin, 1978), pp. 324,
119, 317.

[3] Ibid., p. 325.

mysterious. It is the source of all true
art and science. He to whom this emotion
is a stranger, who can no longer wonder and
stand rapt in awe, is good as dead. His
eyes are closed...To know that what is im-
penetrable to us really exists, manifesting
itself as the highest wisdom and the most
radiant beauty which our dull facilities
can comprehend only in the most primitive
forms--this knowledge, this feeling, is at
the center of true religiousness. In this
sense, and in this sense only, I belong to
the ranks of the devoutly religious men."[4]

The end of the cosmos is a popular subject for
movies and writers today. One of the most famous
theories is that of the Hubble constant. "According
to the theory of the expanding universe, the red
shifts observed in the spectra of stars in external
galaxies represent recessional velocities...If the
universe had been expanding at a constant rate...the
upper limit to its age would be 20 times $10^9$ years."[5]

This upper limit, in billions of years, is not
especially fearful. We can hardly conceive of such a
period of time. Only astronomers, physicists, and
mathematicians think in those terms. Einstein's "un-
attainable," with its awesome beauty, is inherent in
this vision.

Modern scientists and engineers introduced the
Space Age. Their discoveries and those which inspired
them brought man to the moon and led to the orbiting
spaceships of Russia and the United States. It is easy
to oversimplify this scientific and technical lineage.
Nevertheless, it was their work which fructified
thoughts of brilliant astrophysicists and technicians
and enabled our space adventurers to reach the moon and
to get close to Jupiter and other distant planets.

The universe, as Einstein asserted, is closed. As
we have seen, Friedman and Einstein predicted that the
universe itself is dynamic. This is now a core of modern physics.

---

[4] Albert Einstein, What I Believe, 1930.
[5] Valerie H. Pitt, ed., op.cit., p. 183.

According to certain recent theorists, the core of a white dwarf star suffers a gravitational collapse. This forms a neutron star of greater density. Temporarily, the collapse may slow, with neutron-star densities finally being reached. After that, it is foreseen that the collapse will continue and speed up. Matter gets more and more compact. Then a horizon forms and a black hole begins. Gravitational collapse is among modern physics' astonishing predictions. It has been asserted that general relativity is one of the most extraordinary concepts of all physics.

Einstein's forecasts were momentous: every closed model universe, even the most irregular, shows inevitability of gravitational collapse. This precept is included in standard relativity as an accepted prediction.

The heart of modern physics is its ultimate mutability. With all other laws of physics considered as mutable, the evolution of quantum physics from classical physics is a prime example of that mutability. The world of physics as a fixed science is drastically altered by the quantum principle. The observer must reach in, put in the equipment he needs for measurement. The measurement changes the state of the electron. Thereafter the universe is changed. The measurer is a participator, therefore the universe is a participatory universe. Every person who measures changes what is being measured. This means that the universe is being measured and changed constantly.

"Are we," as Thomas Mann said, "actually bringing about what seems to be happening?"[6]

We, as observer-measurers, stir ever so slightly into elements of the universe. We wave our hands in the wind; we thereby change the velocity of the wind. We tread the earth; it changes composition under our steps. Someone measures a sponge. It increases almost imperceptibly in length. What is happening? Those of us who act on nature transform it. Mutability is everywhere latent.

---

6 John A. Wheeler, "From Relativity to Mutability," in Jagdish Mehra, The Physicist's Conception of Nature (Boston: Reidel, 1973), p. 244.

As John A. Wheeler has stated, "Mutability and collapse strain judgment. It is sure that physics itself can never again explain physics.[7]

The stellar universe is expanding. Light from distant stars shows the Doppler effect: the wave lengths in the spectra are shifted toward the red. Thus the stars are receding from the center of the universe. As the distance away from the center increases, this "red shift" becomes larger, thus pointing to an "exploding universe."

Unheard-of expansion of our cosmos is a new, astonishing fact. As the stars recede away from the core of the universe, possibilities for explosion of the cosmos increase. Dramatists in France since 1900 have been more and more aware that the final destiny of our universe is precarious, in fact doomed. Ionesco's La Colère (Anger, 1963) is the prime example. After a husband-wife argument over soup, riot begins in the streets, then war, then world war, and at last our planet blows up.

The German-Swiss dramatist, Friedrich Dürrenmatt, presaged atomic and post-atomic explosiveness in world strata in The Physicists (1961). Dangerous games are played. Several scientists, masquerading under assumed names of famous historical figures, vie with each other for the control of atomic secrets. Murder is one perverse consequence.

If one calculated back in time, he could conclude, in one estimate, that all of the galaxies in the universe were crowded together in space about 10-15 billion years ago. With the enormous condensation of matter now known, the laws of physics would predict that there would be a gigantic explosion of the condensed matter. Hence the receding galaxies might correspond to the pieces of an exploding grenade. This is the "Big Bang" theory of the expanding universe.

"The Big Bang Theory is a theory in cosmology postulating that at some time about 10 times $10^9$ years ago

---

[7] Ibid., p. 244.

all the matter of the universe was packed into a super-
dense small agglomeration subsequently being hurled in
all directions at enormous speeds by a cataclysmic explosion."[8]

The expansion of our universe is now documented.

Lines in the spectrum of light from remote
galaxies are shifted toward the long wave-
length end by an amount which is greatest
for those nebulae believed to be farthest
away. If this red shift is interpreted as
due to a velocity away from the earth in the
line of sight, then those galaxies that are
farthest away are moving fastest. Thus the
universe appears to be expanding.[9]

Various evidence suggests strongly that our cosmos
is growing and changing. Light, by its spectra, proves
this idea. Remote galaxies, in the way they send out
rays of light, provide evidence. As these galaxies
move faster and faster away from the earth, these
stars suggest the expansion of our cosmos.

A "pulsating universe" is a hypothesis. It is con-
ceded that all matter in the universe exploded from a
small nucleus. This expansion continues. Later, will
this matter contract, making the universe become a massive "dark hole"? Will the cycle recommence?

The related Doppler effect can be illustrated by a
common phenomenon: when a train locomotive emits sound
waves (these coming from a moving source) the tone of
the whistle rises as the train approaches an observer.
This is the Doppler effect. From a moving source, light
waves show this identical effect.

This red shift indicates a velocity such that the
speed of the source is approximately proportional to its
distance from the earth. The exploding universe theory
is based partly on this good evidence. It imagines the
universe as having been born several billion years ago
in an immense explosion. (Evidence that the universe
could contract at a later era is not so strong.)

------------------------------

[8] Valerie H. Pitt, op.cit., p. 41.

[9] Ibid., p. 142.

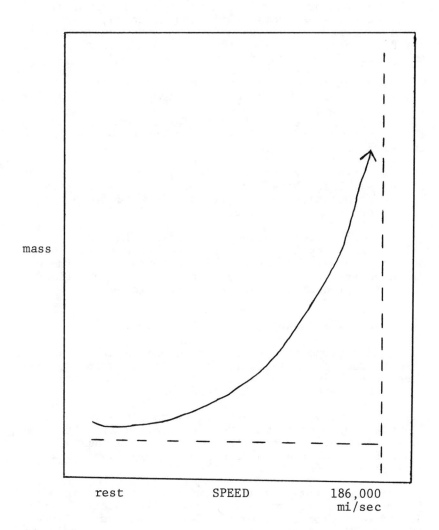

mass

rest                    SPEED                  186,000
                                               mi/sec

The idea of an exploding universe is grandiose. If a closed universe shows gravitational collapse, as Einstein declared, this possibility is announced. Einstein's theories, complex though they may seem, are part and parcel of a large pattern.

The spacetime continuum: Einstein's theory of relativity, by casting doubt on the concept of simultaneity, led to the idea of the three dimensions of space and one of time being taken together to form a reference system. Thus for complete specification an event must be defined in terms for a four-dimensional continuum.[10]

How can one assess the exact location of an object in space? Relativity, in Einsteinian terms, lets us know that no object by itself has either definable location or measurable velocity.

Motion, a related concept, is seen in space-time relationships by Einstein. In order to describe the motion of a particle or a wave the concepts of time and distance are used. These concepts are left undefined as intuitive with universally accepted meanings.

What is a "continuum"?

A continuum (as in space-time continuum) is an area that is continuous and self-same. In relativity mechanics, radically new views of the nature of time and space were developed by Einstein and others.

As we know, Einstein believed that the speed of light in empty space must be identical in all directions, independent of the motion of the source or observer. (This fact led Einstein to his development of the special theory of relativity.)

Probably the most important idea of Einstein's as it was applied to immediate use was the interconvertibility of matter and energy. $E=mc^2$. When a particle of matter is converted to energy (matter into radiation) a tremendous amount of energy is released. This is the basis of nuclear bombs.

---

[10] Valerie H. Pitt, op. cit., p. 157.

As we have said, Einstein was not responsible for the technological advances that went into the development and availability of nuclear bombs. The relationship $E = mc^2$ was the key in spite of Einstein's desires. Matter was converted into energy, with the terrific potential for destruction, maiming, and permanent bodily damage that was realized in the Japanese cities of Hiroshima and Nagasaki.

Time, in its strange manifestations, preoccupied Einstein. One of his most piquant paradoxes was that of the twin space travelers. Space travelers will not age as fast as twin brothers on earth. If a space traveler twin brother could move with the speed of light, he would not age at all in comparison with his twin on earth.

Time slows down for a space traveler. This is an amazing idea. To age not at all, by moving through space at the speed of light: an unrealizable dream. Movies could well feature it. What would twins say to each other if they were able to speak over an ultramodern communications system? The one on earth speaking of age's coming, the one in a space ship blithely assuming that time had stopped.

To understand space travel, we need to know the qualities of velocity. The negative result of the Michelson-Morley experiments was interpreted by Einstein as indicating that absolute velocity cannot be measured but rather only relative velocity.

The special theory of relativity (1905) dealt only with reference systems moving at constant velocity relative to each other.

The special theory of relativity was based on two postulates: (1) The laws of physical phenomena are the same in either of two reference systems moving with constant velocity relative to each other. (2) The velocity of light in empty space is the same for all observers and is independent of the light source relative to the observer. If two events take place simultaneously at different locations it is not possible to say which of the two precedes the other or that they occur simultaneously.

Absolute velocity cannot be measured. It is relative. Absolute simultaneity is impossible to determine.

If two events are at different locations, their simultaneity or lack of it is unmeasurable in the absolute. Playwrights in modern France instinctively have rejected absolutes in timing and in location.

In Jean Anouilh's Thieves' Carnival (1938),[11] the plot is based on upside-down timing. The clever comedy is a flight from time, a sort of theatrical fugue. Let us recall that the fugue, in music, is the consummate form of the polyphonic style of composition, requiring a mastery of all the devices of counterpoint.

Fugue: a polyphonic composition based on one, two, or even more themes, which are enunciated by the several voices or parts in turn, subjected to various kinds of contrapuntal treatment, and gradually built up into a complex form having somewhat distinct divisions or stages of development and a marked climax at the end.

Strict fugue: each division symmetrical, purely contrapuntal.

Free fugue: irregular and incomplete in plan or detail.

In the conclusion, the theme is presented by all the voices in turn.


Thieves' Carnival is a free theatrical fugue and a somewhat involuted play of illusions, in which time plays a bedazzling role. Rhythm and velocity of action are decisive.

Esthetically, this is the problem: Is the charm of illusion more beautiful and more valuable than the blandishments of material reality?

Two pairs of lovers whirl temporally, backwards and forwards. Gustave-Juliette, Hector-Eva. Muted drama results. Gustave and Hector are thieves, led by the crafty Peterbono. As they calculate strategies to rob

---

11 Jean Anouilh, Le Bal des voleurs (Thieves' Carnival) (Paris: Livre de Poche, 1958).

Lord Edgard and Lady Hurf, along with their nieces Eva
and Juliette, love strikes.

Lady Hurf, meneuse de jeu, getting on in years,
filters time into fine grains. Her role in the fugue
is to dream. Romance of other years, romance today.

Speaking to Lord Edgard, Lady Hurf spins revery:

Lady Hurf: Understand me. Here we are in charge
of souls. Now, intrigues are being woven;
marriages are being prepared. Personally, I
can't follow them. That gives me the migraine.
Who will be supposed to penetrate them,
direct them?

Lord Edgard: Who?[12]

Lady Hurf is caught up in the web of time. Events
are moving too fast for her. Eva and Hector, Gustave
and Juliette, falling in and out of love, are rhythmi-
cally too advanced for her tempo of other years.

A few minutes before, Lady Hurf had questioned
Lord Edgard:

Lady Hurf: Well now, my dear Edgard, what
have you done during this day?

Lord Edgard: ...I..I..I read the Times.

Lady Hurf, severe: The same as yesterday?

Lord Edgard, ingenuous: Not the same number
as yesterday.

Hector, who was observing, whistles in admiration:
Did you see the pearls?

Peterbono: Four million.

Hector: Shall we go ahead? Russian prince?

Peterbono: No. She seems to know what's
going on. Ruined Spaniards.[13]

---

12 Jean Anouilh, Ibid., p. 145.
13 Ibid., p. 144.

The love affair Eva-Hector had begun well.  His
face managed to please her.  Later, it turns badly.
Hector is in despair:

Hector:  Ah! Why can't I succeed in pleasing
you a second time?

Eva:  You know very well, you're not the same
person.

Hector:  What a horrible absence of memory!
I told you, this disguise was a fantasy of an
harassed aristocrat concerning his personality,
one who finds his amusement in that way to
escape from himself.  I can't, because of
this cursed fantasy, lose my love, Eva!

Eva:  I conserve with pleasure the recollection
of a young man who spoke to me in the park.
Find him again.  Perhaps I'll be in love with
him again.

Hector:  Ah!  What a ridiculous adventure!
If you only consented to put me on the track.
Just tell me if I had a beard when I pleased
you.

Eva:  I already answered you that it wouldn't
amuse me any more if I told you.

Hector:  who has turned around to change his
visage and who appears, completely different:
It wasn't this way.

Eva bursts out in laughter:  Oh! No...

Hector:  You recognize my voice, my eyes
nevertheless?

Eva:  Yes, but that isn't enough.

Hector:  I have the same figure!  I am tall,
well built.  I assure you that I am well built.

Eva:  I only believe in faces.

Hector:  That's horrible!  That's horrible!
I'll never find again in what form I pleased
you.[14]

58

The net of time, with its transitoriness and its sweeping along as though willy-nilly toward old age are Lady Hurf's drama. She tries to live in other days but also simultaneously by getting wind of the romances of Eva and Juliette. Nothing can be done. She nearly faces this. False simultaneity, unlike the near-simultaneities posed by Einstein, is her psychic undoing. Situations of love are never similar. Eva and, somewhat like her, Juliette, maneuver for themselves, in frustration.

Hector's upset is both comic and sad. While in only one false disguise had he found agreement in Eva. Love is timely; it cannot be nurtured on incognito or in camouflage; and it must have the marvelous timing that happens only too rarely.

As Hector tries to rediscover the guise in which he found Eva's favor, using countenance after countenance, mustache after mustache (a brilliant piece of drama by Anouilh), he symbolizes an almost Pirandellian comic search for definable identity. Time is against him. Time, relative but demonstrable, tricks him into loss of his love.

Einstein's relativity of time, in terms of physics, is counterpointed by a sparkling temporal relativity in the case of Eva and Hector. They seem to be made for each other in the beginning; their fate turns sour, for Eva's rejection of Hector is relative to a new time, a completely or almost completely new situation. Relativity is in Eva's disillusioned eye; it is the eye of the beholder.

Time's reversals entrap Hector. The present moment is fluid. He desperately does what he can to make the past (Eva's pleasure in meeting him) resurge as actuality, now. Impossible. Anouilh's technique is not that of a Hollywood flashback. It is more subtle. Hector is living flashes of his previous existence, convoluted and twisted. What he wants he cannot have.

The finesse of this scene is considerable. We glimpse Hector's evolution, thief and lover, or would-be lover, from the earliest point in the play to the moment

---

14 Ibid., 167-168.

when Eva tells him that love is futile; it has gone.
Nor can he find his true form.  Pirandello is here, in
powerful suggestivity.

Anouilh's beautiful conclusion is:  Can freedom
created by voluntary illusion be more valuable than
freedom obtained in social reality?  The puzzle is set.

Already mentioned, Heisenberg's principle is of
paramount importance.  It is called the indeterminacy
principle.  It reveals the consequence of the fact that
any measurement of a system must disturb it, with a re-
sulting lack of precision in measurement.  The principle is of fundamental importance in the behavior of
systems on the atomic scale.[15]

Heisenberg attributed the original inspiration in
formulating the uncertainty principle to a conversation
that he had with Einstein in 1926.  One vital consequence of uncertainty is that the laws of physics have
to be statistical in character.[16]

As we have seen, Heisenberg's principle converts
the laws of physics into relative probabilities instead
of absolute certainties.  Measurement is, in the end,
indecisive.  In many French plays of the modern period,
a kind of systematic indecisiveness is the rule.  Conclusions are no longer settled and clear; irresolution
comes to the fore.  In Anouilh's Le Bal des voleurs,
a prime instance, the young lovers are left vibrating,
lost from certainty.

As far as time is concerned, Einstein's notion was
straightforward:  "The notion of time itself arises initially in our everyday experience by watching sequences
of events happening in one locality, rather than in all
of space."[17]

---

15 Valerie H. Pitt, op.cit., p. 396.

16 B. K. Ridley, Time, Space and Things (Harmonds-
woth: Penguin, 1976), p. 102.

17 Albert Einstein, Relativity: the Special and the
General Theory (New York: Crown, 1961), p. 75.

Even more upsetting outlooks on time have come along. B. K. Ridley avers, "In spite of the strong impression of time as something flowing ever onward, there is nothing in the laws of motion, be they mechanical or electromagnetic, which differentiates between time running forward or backward."[18]

The flow of time in surrealistic plays during the 1920's in France was at times irregular, gushing out like a fountain which stops and starts. Even the avant-garde, pre-surrealistic play by Guillaume Apollinaire, Les Mamelles de Tiresias (1917) came close to this concept, when the husband produced thousands of babies in one day. Time was topsy-turvy throughout.

Perhaps the most enduring of the surrealist playwrights, Roger Vitrac, was imagined telling his wife when he was approaching middle age, "You'll see, how I'll be young!" His outstanding plays reflected this yearning, as did a large number of Jean Anouilh's. Turn the clock backwards, make time flow in reverse. In Les Mystères de l'amour, (1927) Vitrac confronts diurnal activity and dream. Elapsed time loses its validity, as a new method of progression on stage takes over.

Victor ou les Enfants au Pouvoir (Victor or Children to Power), 1928,[19] Vitrac's undoubted masterpiece, features a boy-giant, Victor. He tongue-lashes society for its vices and ills. He has grown much too fast, much too smart. The drama is one of a sharp generation gap. Victor is prescient; he sees the future as it may develop. In the end, he dies, victim of his relatives and friends, who are befuddled about how to handle this all-knowing young giant.

In the expanding universe, says B.K. Ridley, if time increases so does the distance between galaxies.[20]

The known universe is the jack-in-the-box of every adventurous young author of plays, in France as else-

---

[18] B. K. Ridley, op.cit., pp. 62-63.

[19] Roger Vitrac, Victor ou les enfants au pouvoir, in Robert B. Marshall and Frederic C. St. Aubyn, Trois pièces surréalistes (New York: Appleton-Century Crofts, 1969).

[20] B. K. Ridley, op. cit., p. 63.

where. Armand Gatti, in Chroniques d'une planète pro-
visoire (1962) investigates the problems of earthlings
who engage in hostilities on a new planet. Not too sur-
prisingly, these conflicts are very similar to those the
adventurers had left on earth. For present-day explorers, distances as they increase to faraway stars have
little terror in themselves.

Time, similarly. Today's space shuttle astronauts
wait many long hours inside the space ship before a mis-
sion is scrubbed. Those fatiguing hours hardly seem as
onerous to the astronauts as they would have in regular
duty outside the spacecraft. Time is relative to the
job at hand.

Astronauts are the prototypes of our dream of per-
fected human beings, able to circumnavigate the universe
without physical harm. One day, man may travel in space
somewhat as he flies to Europe for vacation. His body
and mind, steeled for hazards not yet encountered, have
to be assiduously prepared.

A recent book Robots Robots Robots, edited by Harry
M. Deduld and Ronald Gottesman, surveys the advent of
the robot since Karel Capek coined the word until Asimov's I, Robot and beyond. Einstein's vision of a per-
fectible man who would give his spirit to the cause of
world concord and peace may have reached some fruition
in the highly skilled astronauts, who exclaimed in wonder at viewing Mother Earth from thousands of miles
away in space, and cried out happily: one played golf
when they set foot on the moon for the first time.

Ann Trivisonno, in an article on the esthetics of
Samuel Beckett, noted:

> Poetry was the first operation of the human
> mind, and without it thought could not exist.
> Barbarians, incapable of analysis and abstrac-
> tion, must use their fantasy to explain what
> their reason cannot comprehend. Before ar-
> ticulation comes song; before abstract terms,
> metaphors. The figurative character of the
> oldest poetry must be regarded, not as sophi-
> sticated confectionery, but as evidence of a
> poverty-stricken vocabulary and of a disability
> to achieve abstraction. Poetry is essentially
> the antithesis of Metaphysics: Metaphysics
> purges the mind of the senses and cultivates

the disembodiment of the spiritual; Poetry is
all passion and feeling and animates the in-
animate; Metaphysics are most perfect when
most concerned with universals; Poetry when
most concerned with particulars.

The poetics of space exploration today and tomorrow,
when astronauts find colorful and imaginative terms to
describe the moon or their view of the earth, are joined
with all the physics and mathematics they had to learn
before embarking on space travel. Poetry is indeed
elemental. Its particulars laud the Maker; at the same
time the finicky details of the technological flights
take on forms of poetry. In space voyages, science and
literature are intellectual bedfellows.

I have discussed Hubble's Law, one of the crucial
statements in modern astrophysics. In the 1930's, the
astronomer Edwin Hubble derived a relation between the
distance of galaxies and the speed at which they were
moving away from the earth. This relation, known as
Hubble's Law, states that very distant objects are
moving away from Earth faster than relatively close objects. Astronomers have used Hubble's Law to estimate
the age of the universe as being about 15 to 18 billion
years old, the age depending on a number called Hubble's
constant.

Recently, three scientists have found a possible
error in Hubble's constant, and their new value is
twice as large as the old one. This means the universe
may be only 9 billion years old. The new value has not
been accepted, but if these scientists are correct,
astronomers may be faced with some new problems including the age of stars.

Science, never final, changes, sometimes radically.
Hubble's constant, so fascinating because when we tried
to see how old our Cosmos is, we may have been mistaken
in part.

Today, we are told that the known universe is expanding at the rate of some 40 trillion light-years per
second. The quantity is more than prodigious; the idea
is amazing. Not only is our physical universe physical-
ly expanding, but our understanding of it is undergoing
an unprecedented growth as well.

Once exposed to these concepts describing the ex-

plosive nature of our universe, it is no wonder that
modern French playwrights have been impressed.

Already mentioned, Eugene Ionesco's Anger (1963) is
apocalyptic in its comic extravagance. Eating soup, a
husband and wife quarrel over nothings. The spat gets
hotter. Outside the room, in the street, riots begin
to break out. Then wars, localized but rabid. World
War. War spreading everywhere. The final blow: gigantic explosion of the world. The proliferation and
expansivity of armed conflict are remarkable. Ionesco
has always feared the proliferating, madly-out-of-con-
trol phenomena of human existence. The Bald Soprano
(1953) and The Lesson (1953) unleashed the maddening
forces of explosive language and inanity (in the first
play) and murderous, madcap philology roaming willy-
nilly through the hotbeds of foreign languages, fake
and real, in The Lesson.

Ionesco is the modern dramatist par excellence of
total explosiveness. Few other playwrights have been so
bold in predicting how our microcosmic and macrocosmic
worlds will end in a shattering cataclysm.

Yet our worlds, our galaxies persist. "On March
5, 1979, the spacecraft Voyager I detected eight vol-
canic eruptions on the Jovian moon Io in the course of
its historic encounter with Jupiter."[21]

The decade of the 1970's will be remembered as
the golden age of planetary exploration. Mercury,
Venus, Mars, Jupiter, all yielded some of their
remoteness and their secrets to the expanding
curiosity of our species and the instruments of
our robot spacecraft. And now, at the decade's
end, Saturn has succumbed too--the last of the
planets known by the naked eye to the ancient
world. Appropriately enough on Saturday
(Saturn's day), September 1 (1979), the
Pioneer II spacecraft made a two-hour transit
around the sixth planet and passed twice through
its splendid rings.[22]

[21] Scientific American, January 1980, Vol. 242,
no. 1, p. 5.

[22] "Saturn," Science 80, November/December 1979,
p. 24.

As Einstein knew, man's ingenuity, his sharp curiosity, and his perseverance in discovery are almost unlimited. Physics and astronomy hurtle ahead, breathtaking in their speed and majesty. Einstein could hardly have dreamed of what lay ahead in the findings of astrophysics. By and large, his theories of the universe are still valid.

Cosmologists still have plenty of time to debate the question, but the latest clue from outer space suggests that the universe will go on expanding forever and not fall back on itself.

The clue comes from an x-ray satellite aptly named Einstein, and concerns the amount of mass in the universe. Whether the universe eventually collapses depends on how much mass there is to create the gravitational forces that fight expansion. According to current estimates, the matter in all the galaxies is not enough to overcome the outward drift left over from the original Big Bang. But some scientists theorize that the additional mass needed might be found in vast clouds of gas between the galaxies.[23]

Einstein's influence is still clear. An X-ray satellite is named after him. The Big Bang theory of the origin of the universe, as I have mentioned, asserts that some 10 to 15 billion years ago, all the galaxies in the universe were massed in a small space. This is terrific condensation of matter. This is the Big Bang theory of the expanding universe.

If recent scientific findings are accurate, it is possible that our universe will go on living, billions of years from now, contrary to expectations of earlier researchers. Shall we breathe easier?

Basic to all of Einstein's theories was his principle of gravitation. He explained it simply. For example: A man in an elevator which is falling completely free. The man observes that he appears to be "weightless." If he were hanging from a spring balance, it would read zero. (On television, very recently, we

---

[23] "Runaway Universe," Ibid., p. 7.

65

have seen our American astronauts in the space shuttle floating around inside, seemingly "weightless."

The astronaut in a circular orbit around the earth appears to be "weightless." Actually, he is being accelerated toward the earth with the acceleration g, as a result of gravity...Technically this means that there is no way to distinguish between a gravitational field and a region in an accelerated reference system.

Gravitational forces are primordial, nearly inescapable. In drama, there are quite different basic drives. Love, death, ambition, skullduggery, desire, jealousy, friendship, age and aging, fun, and a whole gamut of human feelings are of course the basis of good plays. In combination, if a playwright is very skillful, they impress us with something like the physical-psychic manifestations that physics delineates. Such analogies are not close. But they do exist. Physics, as in gravitation, tells us what happens to matter under prescribed conditions.

Nora, in A Doll's House, is impelled by longing to break free, to find herself independent of hearth and husband. The longing is ultra-modern. It is her moral gravitation. Admittedly, its subtleties differ from anything an Einstein characterized. The far-fetched parallel, nevertheless, is a prototype worth examining.

The impelling powers in modern French plays, as disparate as they are, can be compared at least in minor part to those gravitational forces of which Einstein wrote.

Samuel Beckett's Endgame,[24] one of the most dreary of all celebrated dramas in recent years, is a prelude to death. Death is omnipresent; it pulls, it heaves. It leers. Two leading characters, Hamm and Clov, are in a semi-moribund state, expecting death at any juncture. Hamm, the leader in this macabre ritual, tells Clov, "It's the end, Clov, we've come to the end, I don't need you any more."[25]

---

[24] Samuel Beckett, Endgame (New York: Grove, 1958), p. 79.

[25] Ibid., p. 79.

Hamm: Stop! ...Hamm lays his hand against the
wall. Old wall! (Pause.)
Beyond is the...other hell. (Pause. Violently.)
Closer! Closer! Up against!26

Hamm is a ringmaster of doom. The other hell beyond the wall, beyond the vapid life he knows, is a
net, an executioner's gibbet. Other is the key word.
Existence in the here and now drags on, dire, forlorn,
full of sad tricks. The other world offers nothing
but torture. Hamm and Clov are moved in tiny circles
by a power they cannot resist, gravitation-like. It
is despair, ringlet that is choking them steadily, on
and on, to the death of them. Physical forces have
weighed down Hamm and Clov to the point where death is
believed to be an escape.


Einstein found that an accelerated frame of reference (coordinate system) and a gravitational field
are really two aspects of the same thing.

One cannot experimentally distinguish between them;
therefore it makes no sense to try to consider them as
different. This is called the Principle of Equivalence.
If one accepts this theory he is led to the assumption
that space is in general non-Euclidean.

One concept arising from this theory is the idea
of a black hole.

This is the region in which a massive star has collapsed to the point where its density is so enormous
(a thousand million million times that of water) that
gravitational interactions prevent any radiation from
escaping from the black hole.

People today are unusually intrigued by the visions
they may have of a black hole. Fright, spurred by curiosity, is their reaction. Hollywood has profited by
this rather gruesome inquisitiveness. At least one movie dealing with adventures of space explorers going too
close to a black hole has been made.

Nature's fickleness was noted by Einstein. "Both
space and time are equally fickle and depend on the

---

26 Ibid., pp. 25-26.

relative motion of observers."[27]

    If Nature is capricious, so is man. This is a dictum. Yet it is worth repeating. A staple of modern drama, as well as ancient, is infidelity. Mozart's well-known opera, Cosi fan tutte, is a scintillating masterpiece devoted mainly to fickleness.

    Time and space are interrelated, as Einstein proved. The geometry of space is changing with time.

    Two of the most powerful concepts of our era, those defining space and time, have been shown by Einstein to intertwine, losing distinctiveness. How have modern French playwrights staged this interrelationship? Integral to a certain number of important plays since 1896, it is embodied with wit and pungency in works by Ionesco, Beckett, Jarry, Apollinaire, and others. It remains to be seen exactly how each author discovered his own formula.

[27] Albert Einstein, quoted in "The Year of Doctor Einstein," Time, February 19, 1979, p. 73.

CHAPTER V

A famous pronouncement occurs in Hamlet: "The
time is out of joint."[1] Both time and space are likewise disjointed, piecemeal, topsy-turvy, in Alfred
Jarry's Ubu Roi (Ubu the King) (1896). A comic Tzar
falls into a ditch, in a wild scene which is a prelude
to another extravaganza in the snow of Lithuania. "An
inexplicable terror to attack and annul in us the effects of our courage," Ubu exclaims.[2]

A few moments later, a Polish friend yells, "Flee
for your lives." Ubu answers, "Come on! On our way.
What a pile of people, what a multitude, how will I
ever get myself out of this mess?"[3]

Disemboweled time (for the rational idea of time
seldom comes to mind in Ubu) and the mess, the mishmash
of how time is to progress. Space, concurrently, becomes a shadow, a figment of nothingness. Ubu and his
fellow conspirators move as in a raw nightmare, jumping
from place to place. Lithuania is but a pretext, not a
true geographical site. Shades of Napoleon's Russian
campaigns in the roiling snow abound, irresistible.

In Act V, the final act of this monstrous comedy,
Mother Ubu screeches, "At last, I have found shelter.
I am alone here, and that's OK, but what a frantic
trip: to have crossed all of Poland in four days!"[4]

Afoot, alone, Mother Ubu has miraculously traversed
the entire width of Poland in four days. This is a decisive indication that Jarry intended to scramble space
and time. In fact, Ubu the King mingles the two ideas
in a dizzying amalgam of the temporal and the spatial.
The entire play, based on this technique, is bewilder-

---

1 Shakespeare, Hamlet (ed. Willard Farnham) (Balti-
  more: Penguin, 1969), Act I, sc. 5, p. 61.

2 Alfred Jarry, Ubu Roi, in Tout Ubu (ed. Maurice
  Saillet) (Paris: Librairie Générale française,
  1962), p. 101.

3 Ibid., p. 102.

4 Ibid., p. 113.

ing. At its initial performance in Paris at the Théâtre de l'Oeuvre on December 10, 1896, the work was hissed at its first exclamation, "Merdre!," and a huge riot ensued in the theatre, preventing the continuation of the play for about fifteen minutes.

Jarry described his setting:

> In any case we have a perfect decor, for just as one good way of setting a play in Eternity is to have revolvers shot off in the year 1000, you will see doors open on fields of snow under blue skies, fireplaces furnished with clocks and swinging wide to serve as doors, and palm trees growing at the foot of a bed so that little elephants standing on bookshelves can browse on them. ...The action, which is about to begin, takes place in Poland, that is to say:  Nowhere.[5]

A scurrilous farce taking place <u>nowhere</u>.  Space is turned in derision.  Poland is a sham, a name on nothing.  So is Lithuania.  Time is eclipsed.  An Eternity of Nowhere, in Roger Shattuck's phrase.  No one other than Jarry could have ventured this and succeeded.  The play is a success in history.  It is a forerunner of surrealism and much of modern theatre.  Shattered are time and space, as poetic figures.  What remains is extravagant tomfoolery, tomfoolery which has cutting depths of sarcasm and truth.

As the play is about to end, a few conspirators are left in a ship, headed toward an enigmatic destination. No one really knows precisely where they are going. The Commander exclaims, "Ah! What a beautiful breeze!" Ubu responds, "It is true that we are flying ahead with a rapidity which is nothing short of prodigious.  We must be making at least a million knots an hour..."[6]

Unheard-of-speed, vaguely recalling Einstein's speed of light.  Fantasy rules.  No one is now supposed to pay attention to mundane preoccupations of space or time.  They do not exist.

---

5 Alfred Jarry, cited in Roger Shattuck, <u>The Banquet Years</u> (Garden City, N.Y.: Anchor, 1958), p. 205.

6 Alfred Jarry, <u>op. cit.</u>, p. 128.

Nearing some sort of land (who knows where?), the
sailors meditate on where they are arriving:

>     MOTHER UBU:   Ah! What a delight to soon see
> again sweet France, our old friends and our
> château, Mondragon!

>     UBU:   Eh! We'll soon be there.   Momentarily
> we'll arrive beneath Elseneur château.

>     PILE:   I feel cheered up again at the idea
> of once more seeing my dear Spain.

>     ...UBU:   As for me, I'm going to have myself
> proclaimed Master of Finance in Paris.[7]

Jarry is an exceptional playwright. Playing dice
with time and space (France, Denmark by implication, and
Spain are jumbled as a single destination), the voracious
youngster (who wrote first versions of Ubu Roi in his
teens) outdid previous fantaisistes, in part through his
unusual use of near-timelessness and near-spacelessness.


Einstein's theory of relativity is world-famous.
It is not well understood, except by initiates.  Playwrights'functions, quite different from those of a
physicist, are to amuse, to entertain, to instruct, to
baffle sometimes.  Bafflement is peculiarly modern.  The
stage is now an instrument for puzzles, for shock, occasionally for venom.  (Cf. Jean Genet's The Blacks, a be-
wildering panoply of black-white vengeance.)

The eye of today's spectator is trained to wonder,
to suspend judgment.  It is, in a word (without going
too far), relative.  It is not Einsteinian, yet its op-
tics spread widely enough to encompass a panoramic dis-
play of possibilities.  It is hardly ever absolutist.

In down-to-earth parlance, there are kinds of popular relativity too.  In fact, relativity is everywhere.
Smells and odors are relative; we can scarcely give them
precise names.  So are temperatures.  In a bath, various
parts of the skin have different degrees of warmth or
cold.  It is impossible to claim that the body has a

---

7 Ibid., p. 130.

single temperature.  What do playwrights do with this
phenomenon?  Do they treat it directly?  How pervasive
is it?

Everywhere involved, time and motion need clarifi-
cation.  Einstein brought a potent new idea to help.
"In order to have complete description of...motion, we
must specify how the body alters its position with time;
i.e., for every point in the trajectory it must be
stated at what time the body is situated there."

Sage statement.  Motion depends on position in
time.  The idea is not complicated, but it is all-
important.  When authors present characters on stage,
each individual gesture, each movement in any direction
whatsoever, must be finely calibrated to suit the exigencies of a text in which some perspective on time is
involved.

Einstein's renowned observations on light are in
some ways reflected in modern French theatre:

(1)   Nothing could ever exceed the speed of light.
(2)   A metre stick moving at a speed approaching
      that of light would appear to become shorter
      and shorter, approaching zero in length if
      that speed could be reached.
(3)   A clock moving likewise would appear to slow
      and stop as the speed of light is reached.
(4)   The mass of a moving object as measured by
      its inertia, would become infinitely large
      in the limit as the object reached the speed
      of light.

Epiphenomena, in Jean Genet's The Blacks (1958),
follow each other with dizzying speed and unerring
energy.  A masque murder of a multiple character, white,
dazzles spectators with a vengeance of purpose and ritu-
alistic deed new to the French stage.  The faster events
occur, when propelled by a group of blacks, the shorter
their time sequence seems.  Tom Driver has said that the
play is obsessed with energy.  Power, says Bernard
Frechtman, is the true theme of The Blacks.  Raw passion
flows.

Driver tells us:

The play is continually dissolving and then
coming again into shape.  All its depictions are

of epiphenomena. Yet when these disappear we
are not plunged into nothingness. Instead we
descend into a primordial flux of energy out
of which new rituals, oppressions, and re-
venges are born.[8]

It is true that Genet's corrosive drama exudes
vengeful energy. Driving this on in a unique type of
speed; we are hardly conscious of the meanings of what
is happening on stage. Has there been a real murder?
Is it in preparation? Who is (to be) or was the victim? Why? Unanswered questions. The speed of events
in the modern world, possibly foreseen by Einstein in
his famous studies of the speed of light, has changed
man. We exhibit cruelty, spite, hate; we demonstrate
these more rapidly than ever before. In the process,
we "shorten" our time sequence. Space and time, closely
linked, are curtailed. Our hopes are actually abbreviated; our desires limit themselves to aberrant viewpoints, to prejudices. Speed, in human relations, often
misshapes. The analogy with Einstein's concept of the
speed of light is of course indirect and far-fetched.
Yet it is challenging. We wonder.


Proof that Einstein's thoughts are still prevalent
among up-to-date astronomers came in 1979, when the
"Einstein Observatory," an astronomical satellite, was
launched to observe stars and other celestial
phenomena that radiate high-energy X-rays.[9]

Einstein himself might not have anticipated some
of the startling discoveries of modern astronomy, such
as quasars and pulsars. Enigmatic objects called quasars radiate prodigious amounts of energy. They are
visible on earth although they are possibly the most
distant objects in the universe.

Pulsars or neutron stars are also detected. Highly
compressed cadavers of massive stars usually signal
existence by highly regular radio beeps.

---

[8] Tom Driver, Jean Genet (New York: Columbia University Press, 1966), p. 40.

[9] "The Year of Doctor Einstein," Time, February 19,
1979, p. 178.

Astronomers have also picked up what may be the echo of the Creation. Coming from everywhere in the skies, and in a sense from nowhere at all, these faint microwaves appear to be the lingering reverberations of the Big Bang, the cataclysmic explosion in which the universe was apparently born 15 to 20 billion years ago.[10]

One of Einstein's chief contributions to astronomy was his concept of four-dimensional space-time. "And yet there is no more commonplace statement than that the world in which we live is a four-dimensional space-time continuum," wrote Einstein.[11]

The physicist's space-time is defined by three spatial coordinates: horizontal, vertical, and a third dimension in cubic space. Time is the fourth coordinate or dimension.

This is one of Einstein's earth-shaking precepts. The extra dimension of time surprises us. Yet all close observations of our physical and social universe lead us to accept such an idea. We are living in four dimensions. Alfred Jarry's Ubu the King, as I have shown, swallows up these dimensions avariciously. Time is thrown overboard, but it still haunts the Polish conspirators, who cannot escape its tentacles.

In Tiger at the Gates, by Jean Giraudoux, war is beyond time and in time. It is a tiger waiting at the gates, perpetually, so it seems. Yet the characters are bound by the exigencies of instantaneous time.

What is gravity? Einstein declared that it really is a property of space-time. Gravity produces a force between two bodies.

A scientist rides in an elevator in space far from the earth. The elevator accelerates "upward" at a rate of 9.8 meters per second.

Because of his body's resistance to change in velocity (his inertia) his feet press against the floor just as though the elevator were at rest on the earth's surface.

---

10 Ibid., p. 78.
11 Albert Einstein, Relativity: The Special and General Theory (New York: Crown, 1961), p. 55.

He cannot tell whether the force on his feet is gravitational or inertial.

A genius who redefined gravity and the behavior of light, Einstein had a separate life: love of peace and human justice, opposition to anti-Semitism. As a Jew, Einstein had suffered greatly. Israel was a prized land for him. The scientist explained the two sides of his personality: "My scientific work is motivated by an irresistible longing to understand the secrets of nature and by no other feelings.

My love for justice and the striving to contribute towards the improvement of human conditions are quite independent from my scientific interest."[12]

Human justice, divine justice. Einstein believed in God, not a punishing God but "a spirit vastly superior to that of man."

Everyone who is seriously involved in
the pursuit of science becomes convinced that
a spirit is manifest in the laws of the Uni-
verse--a spirit vastly superior to that of
man, and one in the face of which we with our
modest powers must feel humble...
I know from my own painful searching,
with its many blind alleys, how hard it is
to take a reliable step, be it ever so small,
toward the understanding of that which is
truly significant."[13]

Einstein's researchs led him to investigate the nature of matter itself. In his study of Brownian motion, Einstein pointed out that microscopic particles were being jostled by molecules in the liquid.

Einstein helped to discover the phenomena of matter-energy relationships. Few if any scientific findings of our century have surpassed this in importance. Without his knowledge, modern man might have waited many years for atomic energy and the nuclear and hydrogen bombs.

---

12 Albert Einstein, in Ibid., p. 75.

13 Albert Einstein, "The Year of Dr. Einstein," Time (February 19, 1979), p. 75.

Einstein was an expert on energy. One of Einstein's historic findings resulted in the revelations that matter can be converted into energy and thereby its mass will be reduced in accordance with the equation $mass=\dfrac{energy}{(speed\ of\ light)^2}$, $m=\dfrac{E}{c^2}$. This famous Einstein equation also eventually explained why the sun could burn for so many billions of years while shrinking only slightly in size.

French playwrights since 1896, like those of other countries, have recoiled from direct attacks on problems of this size and scope. Some aspects of physics appear to be unassailable. The nuclear bomb, of course, giant myth and reality of our epoch, has been evoked by authors in novel as well as play. But the problem is still too gigantic. It passes human proportions. In France, Gabriel Cousin wrote, in Le drame du Fukuryu Maru, a denunciation of atomic testing by the United States in the Pacific, near a Japanese fishing trawler.

For the play, Albert Einstein wrote a memorable prelude: "The unleashed power of the atom has changed everything, except for our modes of thought, and we are thus slipping toward an unprecedented catastrophe.

A new way of thinking is essential if humanity is to survive."[14]

Here is undeniable evidence that Einstein, humanist as well as scientist, recognized the horrifying dangers inherent in the atom bomb as it was actually dropped and exploded. In writing a message for Gabriel Cousin, whose drama perhaps scared away vast portions of the audiences he might have had, Einstein demonstrated his active interest in a theatrical experience which had direct relationships to his own scientific thought.

Einstein had revised Newton's concept that time is absolute, that it is universally the same, and that it flows steadily from the past toward the future.[15]

---

14 Albert Einstein, message for Gabriel Cousin, Le drame du Fukuryu Maru (Paris: Gallimard, 1960), p. 7.
15 Time, (February 19, 1979), p. 73.

A revision of Newton's idea of absolute length was demonstrated by Einstein. In Einstein's world, time and distance depend on the relative motion of observers.[16]

Among Einstein's other key concepts:

(1) An experiment can detect only relative motion, that is, the motion of one observer with respect to another.
(2) Regardless of the motion of its source, light always moves through empty space at a constant speed.[17]
(3) Intuition is a sacred gift.
(4) In a dazzling world of relativity, ordinary time and space are replaced by baffling effects that seem to differ from common sense.[18]

$E=mc^2$. Mass being converted to energy causes the sun to shine.[19]

A clock in lower orbit will seem to run more slowly than an identical clock in higher orbit, partly because gravity is stronger closer to earth, partly because orbital speed is greater closer to earth.

...An astronaut traveling at high speed with a clock senses no changes, but his twin on earth notes remarkable relativistic effects: the space ship and everything in it have increased in mass and contracted in the direction of travel; the shipboard time has slowed down relative to earth, and the astronaut is aging more slowly.[20]

What have been some of Albert Einstein's influences?

(1) "Einstein's theories tend to become stronger with time." -- Yale physicist Feza Gursey.

(2) Scientists are...conducting ever more sensi-

---

[16] Ibid., p. 73.
[17] Ibid., p. 73.
[18] Ibid., p. 71.
[19] Ibid., p. 71.
[20] Ibid., p. 70.

tive tests of Einstein's theory. M.I.T.'s Shapiro and
his colleagues have been sending radio signals past the
rim of the sun, bouncing them off other planets and
clocking their return to earth to an accuracy much better than a millionth of a second.

The object: to see if solar gravity slows the signals down by the amount forecast by Einstein.

So far, general relativity has passed these and
other tests without exception.[21]

(3) ...We can use the presently accepted theory of
gravitation, Einstein's general theory of relativity, to
convert our present observations into a picture of the
past (and future) history of the universe.

(4) The scenario of cosmic evolution that emerges
can be outlined as follows:

(5) Time can be measured from the instant of the
Big Bang, when all the matter in the universe was in
the form of a uniform gas of particles and radiation at
an unimaginably high temperature and degree of compac-
tion.

(6) The universe is changing with time.

(7) The dramatic evidence supporting a Big Bang
origin of the universe was revealed in 1965 by the most
important cosmological advance of the last half-century:
the discovery of the cosmic microwave radiation.
The Friedman-Einstein prediction that the universe itself is dynamic, in the beginning too incredible for
Einstein himself to believe, has now become a central
fact of modern physics.

(8) With the universe proved dynamic, one is more
ready to accept three other ideas from Einstein's general relativity:

---

[21] Ibid., p. 72.

(a) that other incredible prediction, that
collapse is inevitable, and two prior
ideas,

(b) that the universe is closed;

(c) that geometry is a new dynamic partici-
pant on the stage of physics.

(9) The universe cannot be static.

(10) The volume of a closed model universe is not
constant.

(11) Total energy and total angular momentum cannot
be defined for a closed universe. They are meaningless
concepts.

(12) Einstein transformed the geometrical structure
of spacetime from a rigidly even, never-changing, absolute entity into a variable, dynamical field interacting
with matter.[22]

A shocking, dynamic playwright still living in Paris
is Fernando Arrabal. Geometrically, he veers time and
again into a world of childhood love and perversity.
Fando et Lis (1958),[23] in its outlandish cruelty, is
typical. Eros and Thanatos vie: sexuality, death.
Space crowds in on them. Time's foreshortening is
catastrophic. Though lacking the solidity of ancient
tragedies, Fando et Lis offers a summation of what is
willfully malevolent. Dynamic power courses through the
anti-hero, Fando, who kills his lover, Lis, in the sup-
position that he is sending her to a better life. Bernard Gille asserts that the profound rhythm of Fando et
Lis give it a construction that is quasi-tragic.[24]

[22] Cf. Jagdish Mehra (ed.) The Physicist's Conception of Nature (Boston: Reidel, 1973).
[23] Fernando Arrabal, Fando et Lis, Théâtre I (Paris:
Christian Bourgois, 1958).
[24] Bernard Gille, Arrabal (Paris: Seghers, 1970),
p. 28.

Lis is paralyzed. Fando uses a baby carriage to take her from place to place. Modern sadism enters the picture. Chains, flagellations recall the Marquis de Sade. Pacifying tortures. Arrabal claimed that his play was meant to echo Romeo and Juliet. Mutatis mutandis. Arrabal is a poet-dramatist, far ahead of his day, who vaunts mutability. Morals are designed to be smashed. Arrabal is an iconoclast of dramatics as Einstein was of physics. On a different level, of course. Arrabal, because he loves shock and terror, will never attain wide popularity. Some of his later dramas are very weak and ridden with sensationalism, though his "panic play," L'Architecte et l'Empereur d'Assyrie (1966) stands out in its vibrant, innovative transpositions of characters (one replacing another), and in its impassioned dialogues.

Eugène Ionesco, a former Rumanian now living in Paris, is an intellectual citizen of the world. His theatre is often feverish, boiling with activity. One of his famous plays, The Bald Soprano (1950)[25] is a sort of prelude to Anger, an explosive film scenario of 1963. "Anti-play," The Bald Soprano feeds on mock surfaces of British gentility, wildly parodied. An insidious hero crawls from under the carpet: language. Time and language are at odds. The dynamics of the play, unique in Western civilization, forge ahead under the impetus of pungently satirical word-plays and social commentary. Acceleration is awesome. Martins and Smiths interact in banal words (a maid and a fireman also appear poetically).

In a locomotive-like denouement, with rampaging words taking over the action, language splinters into bits, floating in the air above the heads of the perplexed figurants. At last, a total detonation occurs. Spatial incoherence floods the figurants. Words are shattered. Mental conflagration. Mysteriously, Martins and Smiths interchange bodies in one interpretation.

The Lesson (1951)[26] is a furious, highly kinetic play. A weird professor who claims to be an expert in

---

[25] Eugène Ionesco, La Cantatrice chauve (The Bald Soprano) Theatre I (Paris: Gallimard, 1954).

[26] Eugène Ionesco, La Leçon (The Lesson), Theatre I (Paris: Gallimard, 1954).

the philosophy and interrelationships of languages prepares to receive a feminine student. She is at first timid, loath to go very far in conversation. He turns gradually rabid, like a mad dog, spouting nonsensical vocables of linguistic origin. The whole play is a mad, frenetic crescendo and accelerando, its dynamics rivalling those of discoveries in physics. Mutable. The pace, the timing go mad. Time becomes an ogre.

The young woman turns fearful, suspecting in spite of her naiveté that something is radically amiss. The professor roars on, unwitting of what is about to happen, or seemingly so. This is a wild ritual; we have not been here before, but we smell a perverse odor.

In a culminating outburst of sounds and semi-hypnotic vowels, the professor quasi-mythically seduces an innocent victim. She howls in physical and mental anxiety, as he comes closer. The ending is enigmatic, though clearly violent. It is a calibrated, rapid, figurative rape-murder. Some stagings leave it partly ambiguous. And the professor's maid, a portrait of doom, approaches him, muttering, "Not again. Now you see what can happen." A magic number rolls around in the atmosphere; this is number x in a series of similar murders of the professor's students. Another knock at the door. It is repeated. Next in line, a new female student..


"For us believing physicists the distinction between past, present, and future is only an illusion, even if a stubborn one," Einstein admitted. "God is subtle, but he is not malicious." "If quantum mechanics is true, God is playing dice according to rules known only to him."

Einstein's three pronouncements are essential. The shading of time, denying the strict categories of past, present, and future, is of capital importance. We may be bewildered by such a statement; yet the physics of today and tomorrow and also the theatre in France (as in the United States) works on this assumption, at least in part.

The subtleties of the temporal Godhead, shadowing Old Testament stories of his punishments and harshness, permeate <u>Waiting for Godot</u> (1953). God figures scantily,

but more pervasive is the clash between divine hope and
hopelessness. Two tramps, Vladimir and Estragon, are
central. Vladimir says, "One of the thieves was saved.
That's an honest percentage." A bit later: Vladimir:
"Have you read the Bible?" Estragon: The Bible...
(He reflects.) I must have had a glance at it."
Vladimir (astonished). In the school without God?"[27]

In Waiting for Godot, time nearly stands still.
The adventures of Vladimir and Estragon and of those
who arrive later, Pozzo and Lucky, could take place
almost as well in non-identifiable time. There is a
fuzzy belief that tomorrow will bring the hoped-for
Godot, a puzzling "presence" as indistinct and lacking
in identification as can be imagined. But "tomorrow"
does not really come; the clowns remain walled in
space, in a perpetual semi-timelessness.

Talking to Pozzo, Vladimir asserts, "Time has
stopped."[28] In turn, Estragon expresses a motif of this
extravagant drama: "Nothing takes place, nobody comes,
nobody leaves, it's terrible."[29] Spatially, no major
change is possible.

Somewhat later, Vladimir asks Estragon, "What's
wrong with you?" Estragon: "I am unhappy." Vladimir:
No kidding! Since when?" Estragon: "I had forgotten."[30]

In the second act, still waiting for the unknown
Godot, the two tramps are doing exercises. Estragon
remarks, "You believe that God sees me."[31]

The two have stopped exercising. Estragon: "God
have pity on me!" Vladimir (vexed): "And me?" Estragon (also vexed): "On me! On me! Pity! On me!"[32]

Pozzo, a domineering figure, especially when he

---

[27] Samuel Beckett, En attendant Godot (eds. Germaine Brée and Eric Schoenfeld) (New York:
Macmillan, 1964), pp. 12-13.
[28] Ibid., p. 42.
[29] Ibid., p. 50.
[30] Ibid., pp. 59-60.
[31] Ibid., p. 87.
[32] Ibid., p. 88.

lords it over a slave-like Lucky, exclaims to Vladimir:

You haven't finished poisoning me with
your stories about time? It's senseless!
When! When! One day, isn't that enough
for you, one day just like the others, he
(Lucky) became mute, one day I became blind,
one day we'll become deaf, one day we were
born, one day we'll die, the same day, the
same instant, isn't that enough for you?[33]

This exchange of speeches, quite close to the end
of the play, is a key to the understanding of Beckettian
time. "The same day, the same instant" concept suggests
a curious simultaneity or quasi-simultaneity of dramatic
time. Pozzo protests that all days were and are like
all others. Where are past, present, future? As in
Einstein's theory, Beckett formulates a continuous, virtually indefinable flux. Pozzo rejects talk of time.
He finds it senseless. One day is like all the others.
This is a baffling meaning of Waiting for Godot.


One of Albert Einstein's signal achievements was
linking of explanations of time, space, and gravity.
Among his finest scientific contributions was relating
gravitational forces to the curvature of space. How
did he do his researches? Among the themata which
guided Einstein in theory construction were these:

(1)  primacy of formal (rather than materialistic)
     explanation.

(2)  unity (or unification).

(3)  cosmological scale (generalization and egali-
     tarian application of laws throughout the
     total realm of experience).

(4)  logical parsimony and necessity.

(5)  symmetry.

---

[33] Ibid., p. 104.

(6) simplicity.

(7) causality.

(8) completeness.

(9) continuum.

(10) constancy.

(11) invariance.


God's subtlety, as Einstein saw it, was pursued in his own system of research. Form, as we now know, is universal. In a paradox, completeness becomes part of divine simplicity. In Waiting for Godot, some seventy per cent of the dialogue, in particular that between Vladimir and Estragon, is on all surfaces simple and almost limpid. We have cited Vladimir's question to Estragon referring to the non-secular character of French schools. "In the school without God?" Simple remarks can be profound. Beckett followed Einstein's method of a continuum. His memorable play, misunderstood by early spectators, is basically a continuum, without the marked overturnings which provide finales in traditional theatre.

How can a playwright pretend to emulate Einstein's practice of doing research, when possible, on a "cosmological scale"? Few have done it. Perhaps Eugène Ionesco, one of the most illustrious dramatists in the Western world today, is the best exemplar. In Anger (1963),[34] the French author tackled the question of universal stability. Anger is a very short film scenario. It, like Einstein's recipe for investigation, uses primacy of form, unity, logical parsimony and necessity, symmetry, simplicity, causality, continuum, constancy, and invariance.

---

[34] Eugène Ionesco, La Colère, Théâtre III (Paris: Gallimard, 1963).

A husband and wife dine quietly in a provincial city. Soup. At first, joyous images, inside and out. Love scene: my dove, my pigeon, my rabbit, my lamb, my little cat, my quail, my chicken, my squirrel, my little cabbage, my flower, my crud. Then, a fly in the soup. Recriminations. Accusations. More accusations. A husband throws the contents of his soup bowl at his wife's head.

Same scenes in other apartments. Fatally, blows. Everywhere, blows. Fire in the house. Battles among spouses. The house burns. Riot engaging police and citizens. Tanks in Berlin against workers. Brawls in South Africa among Blacks and Whites. Immense fires. Now war: Hitler, Mussolini. Bombardments of London and Hamburg. Then events which are unleashed: floods, earthquakes, finally reaching the explosion of the atomic bomb. The planet explodes. "Ladies and gentlemen, in a few instants it will be the end of the world."

Last picture: the planet exploding.[35]

An ascending continuum of love pats toward warfare constitutes Anger. After only eight pages, the earth explodes. By implication, according to the necessity of the play's structure, both simple and proliferating, the entire cosmos is next in line to be completely shattered. Where are space and time? Disappearing. The effect of this most unusual film scenario, very little known outside France, is one of love's primacies evolving into violence, of a peaceful small city in the French provinces evolving into the battleground of the world.

So Einsteinian thought percolates into the mental investigations of decades, attaining more or less directly playwrights like Anouilh, Giraudoux, Beckett, Arrabal, and Ionesco. It is difficult to distinguish between thought which playwrights have somehow gotten wind of (in many cases without reading Einstein or other physicists) and ideas which are in the intellectual air, ideas at times irresistible to a young artist in Paris.

---

35 Eugène Ionesco, Ibid., pp. 297-304.

# CHAPTER VI--CONCLUSION

Einstein insisted on the fundamental dualism between experience and theory. In modern French drama, as in theoretical essays and books by critics who too often regard their own opinions highly, this dichotomy is sharp. The structuralists, among the most categorical, and the semioticians, only slightly less so, have vaunted theory, too frequently at the expense of the literary artifacts themselves. In drama, where is experience? On stage, for a relatively few moments, behind footlights of magic or near-necromancy. No theory suffices to explain the action, the color and glitter, the gestures and movement, of a live performance.

The Einsteinian split--experience versus theory--therefore is viable. It is notable that it applies pertinently to the theatre as well as to physics.

On questions of time, as almost always, Einstein was cogent. "The notion of time itself arises initially in our everyday experience by watching sequences of events happening in one locality, rather than in all of space."[1]

The idea of sequences of events that take place in one locality, rather than in all of space, comes rather close to defining much dramatic action. Those sequences, unfolding backwards, giving a static feeling, or proceeding forwards, produce a theatrical sensation. They are the theatrical sensation. Ultra-modern techniques of staging, using advanced types of machinery, lighting, and decor, show rapidly-changing scenes, sometimes appearing to be simultaneous. Einstein's verdict on our notion of time is not infallible. In the main, however, it is tenable for certain key plays as performed in France since 1896.

"Einstein was aware of a paradox. He was trying to deal with great and complex areas of varied experience;

---

[1] Albert Einstein, cited by Gerald Holtonk, "Constructing a Theory: Einstein's Model," The American Scholar, vol. 48, no. 3 (Summer, 1979), p. 316.

87

and yet he imposed the criteria of looking for "simplicity and economy in the basic assumptions."[2]

Samuel Beckett, as I have said, is a prime prototype in France of a dramatic style built on relative outer simplicity in dialogue and action. In fact, critics have delighted in demonstrating the limpidity and occasional bareness of Beckett's vocabulary and plot bases. Beckett's profundity and esoteric truths derive from a quasi-Einsteinian economy of methods. "Beckett and Ionesco are the only men of science among the dramatists we have," has asserted William Saroyan.[3] Entanglements, disrupting limpidity, occur in Waiting for Godot; for example, Lucky's famous speech, a tour de force for any actor, is convoluted and abstruse in the extreme.

In Fernando Arrabal's Le Tricycle, (1961), Mita and Climando exchange, in a crucial scene, the simplest of words, thinking of a possible suicide by Mita:

Climando: What's happening to you?

Mita: Nothing.

Climando: But nothing out of nothing?

Mita: Yes, nothing of nothing of nothing.

Climando: Oh! My! My! How sad you must be!

Mita: I feel like committing suicide for I'm so very sad.[4] (Translation mine.)

Even more convincing as evidence is the structure of an Arrabal play. Picnic on the Battlefield, as we have seen, is simplistic in its overall pattern. Zapo, soldier at the front, with his parents, M. et Mme Tepan, fantasizes war. An enemy soldier, Zepo, shows up.

---

2 Ibid., p. 325.
3 William Saroyan, "Ionesco," Theatre Arts (July, 1958); reprinted in Cahier des Saisons, No. 15 (Winter, 1959), pp. 207-208.
4 Fernando Arrabal, Le Tricycle, Théâtre (Paris: Julliard, 1961), Act I, P. 109.

There are paso doble dances and nostalgic stories told
by M. Tepan, all accentuating Arrabal's purpose; ridi-
culing war.

A picnic, minutes before all are wiped out by enemy
gunfire, heightens the burlesque aspect of warfare.
This burlesque, simply detailed, is Arrabal's method of
constructing a short, taut satire. The tone is constant,
or nearly so. Partly because of this economical taut-
ness, the drama is a masterpiece.


Albert Einstein preferred visual thinking. If he
visualized a set of equations, leading up to a general
theory such as that of relativity or the speed of light,
seeing an idea as hypothesis had its own validity. This,
naturally, assumes that the necessary evidence and logi-
stical support for working out the presupposition are to
be found, examined, and proved. The process is quite
fascinating. Perhaps only a few of the world's leading
physicists could have emulated Einstein's techniques of
visualization.

In modern French drama, the visual sense is all-
important. Ionesco's The Lesson and Exit the King although strikingly different, each take into consideration a series of dramatic optical effects which determine the intrigue. The professor's rabid gesticula-
tions, implying menace, in The Lesson, are a grave fore-
warning of the disaster to come. The tottering steps of
the king, shown in progressive fashion, in Exit the King,
tell us unequivocally that his approaching death is
finally the real thing, not myth.


Einstein allied geometry and physics. This was an
outstanding venture. Between 1907 and 1915, he gradually recognized that gravity is not a force field
existing beside the inertia-determining world-geometry,
but should itself be considered as an aspect of the
spacetime continuum.

With this second step, Einstein transformed the
geometrical structure of spacetime from a rigidly given,
never•changing, absolute entity into a variable, dynamical field interacting with matter. He thereby removed

a disparity between geometry and physics.[5]

Barriers among disciplines and fields of study, however cherished by traditionalists working in a narrow
band of research, have often proved in modern times to
be artificial and false. Physics and geometry are in
part akin. The theatre uses physics (witness the shattering of shards of language and the transformation of
Martins into Smiths and vice-versa in one scenic interpretation of Ionesco's The Bald Soprano and the trans-
figurations of Genet's characters in The Balcony).
There are countless other examples.

The galaxies are moving away from us--the universe
is expanding. This scientific belief, little known by
John Q. Public, is demonstrated in the Döppler effect,
which states that waves from a source moving away from
us are received at lower frequencies than they were
emitted.

Indirect analogies in modern France have been
cited: most sharply, Ionesco's Anger, a film scenario.
This little-known work enlarges the universe of theatre.
Everything on our planet explodes in the end as a consequence of nuclear cataclysm.

Rapid proliferation, Ionesco's favorite motif, has
also joined expansivity of insight, as I have said.
Both belong to the primary discoveries of physics.
Ionesco, certainly one of the modern era's most brilliant playwrights, sees his world with a literary acuity
and sensitivity, whereas Einstein constructed a partly
new world of physics.

Einstein espoused Janusian thinking. This consists
of actively conceiving at least two opposite, antitheti-
cal concepts or ideas of images simultaneously. These
exist side by side. They are also equally operative.
Here is a formulation that leads to integrated concepts,
images, and creations.

---

[5] D. Riedel, "The Nature and Structure of Space-
time," The Physicist's Conception of Nature
(Jagdish Mehra, ed.) (Boston, Reidel, 1973),
p. 72.

Janusian thinking is usually a "crucial step" that occurs at "a moment of inspiration" during creativity, said Einstein. It is a directed thought process involving active formulation rather than association or bisociation.

Without saying so, a certain number of present-day playwrights in France, as elsewhere, have adopted processes similar to Janusian thinking. Samuel Beckett, in Waiting for Godot, bases action on imponderable contradictions (activity and inactivity, verbal splendor and naivete, laziness and dynamism, convolution and simplicity, tenderness and cruelty, hope and despair, reality and irreality, time and timelessness, poetry and baffling prose, jokes and somber seriousness, horseplay and quiescence). These, not mere tricks or comic relief, are the underlying fabric of the play.

Beckett does not seem to arrive at limpid syntheses. His comedy, by virtue of his genius, and despite the dangling arguments in philosophical and psychic terms, ponders Janusian combinations. Quiescence is a form of mental play. Lucky, in his fantastic monologue, shows the obverse extreme, loquaciousness.

Time bedazzles. It is never over; its past is still with us; its future is in us, nowhere else. In gist, we apprehend time piece by piece, event after event, as Einstein maintained.

Time goes on unsullied; or is it us, in our barest understandings of what has happened, who formulate fragile wisps of temporality, trying to locate what cannot be located perfectly. Time is also perilous. For we are perilous. This is one main message of Waiting for Godot.

The Döppler effect shows that the stars are getting more distant. Stated this way, the idea seems clear-cut, and without complications. Findings in physics, after elaborate experiments, differ radically from the inventivity of playwrights.

If the stars are getting more distant, in astrophysical measurements, so are dramatists' visions of human comportment. Endgame, by Samuel Beckett, goes to the ends of the earthly dilemma psychologically, or rather it tastes the bitter dregs of envisaging life's end. No other playwright has dramatized with so much

91

verve and sarcasm the hated approaches to death. Distance from spectators is also primary. We feel estranged; we are unable to believe that human beings, not artists, might in a comparable situation delve so deep into the anguish of despair. The play is unique. Empathy, except for the type perhaps felt for patients expecting doom any day, is an unknown across-the-stage quantity in Endgame. The usual theatrical illusion, its screen filtering out scenic behavior toward ours, is in many ways broken. On stage, near-skeletons; in the audience, living and breathing men and women.

Einstein was a great innovator. "He found the theory of electro-dynamics in disarray and put it on a reasonable and logical foundation that incidentally revolutionized our notions of matter and energy and physical dimensions."[6]

Radical innovators, too, have been Eugene Ionesco, Samuel Beckett, and Fernando Arrabal (the latter less successfully). Before they came along, French theatre was partly stagnating. Bold strokes, bold configurations on stage, bold dialogue and characterization were their fortes. They changed the theatre. In literature as in physics, exciting new perceptions based on solid experimental thought are de rigueur if the art is to advance. After Ionesco and Beckett, imitators sprang up throughout Europe and in the United States. None reached the same level. Theatre today owes a great deal to these two giant innovators, whose role in drama is not completely unlike that played years previously by Einstein in science.

"The great variety of the external situations and the narrowness of the momentary content of consciousness bring about a sort of atomizing of the life of every human being," wrote Einstein.[7]

The idea of every human being undergoing a sort of atomizing is impressive. We all want to expand the sub-

---

6 Dietrick E. Thomsen, "Personality, Place, and Physics," Science News, vol. 115, 1979, p. 212.
7 Albert Einstein, Autobiographisches, translated by Paul Arthur Schipp (Autobiographical Notes) (LaSalle and Chicago: Open Court, 1979), p. 56.

stance of our momentary consciousness to encompass unknown facets of imagination and being. Einstein's is a
wise statement.

In Jean Giraudoux's Intermezzo (The Enchanted,
1933)[8] the delicious young teacher, Isabelle, dreams of
an existence purified of daily lack of imagination. A
Specter appears. He may embody the danger of death.
Isabelle becomes infatuated with him. Her mind, con-
sciously and subconsciously, is not for the moment
attuned to this earth.

Nearly caught in the net of the supernatural,
Isabelle does escape from the universe's outer regions.
A mundane chorus composed of the everyday sounds of her
village calls her back to life. How many of us have
experienced something analogous? After a crisis, return
home, site of pragmatics. Something inside us beckons
to open the garage door very, very slowly, moving in a
semi-ritualistic, stately gait. Slow, slow, we move,
headed toward something spiritual and material simultaneously. The slowness is the key. Reality almost
takes shape, tangible, concrete. It is not a final or
conclusive experience; it is a gateway.

Isabelle's suitor, le Controleur, awaits her. She
will not be able to explain. Her "atomizing" of spirit,
her faculties of unbridled imagination, have had their
day. Now to earthly pleasures.


Along with Freud and Marx, Albert Einstein was a
leading propagator of Western thought after World War I.
Few persons have thought about the possibility that a
genius in physics, a form of thinking which is difficult for most of us, could attract analogies more or
less directly in modern French theatre. These analogies,
which exist, are refracted. Very few are immediate in
their consonance. Those which exist are fascinating.

The mysterious, said Einstein, is the source of all
true art and science. Samuel Beckett, Eugène Ionesco,
Fernando Arrabal, Jean Anouilh, and Jean Giraudoux
leave us with an aroma of man's hidden mysteries. This
is a main purpose and effect of their plays. Beauty is
in mystery. Physics and art do not defy this truth.

_____

8 Jean Giraudoux, Intermezzo (Paris: Grasset, 1933).

A few French dramatists have insinuated the mysteriousness of the universe. Samuel Beckett's enigmas lie deep in the human soul. Time challenges us; we never win. Why? Ennui is rife. How to conquer it? Is there salvation? Who can say?

Fernando Arrabal, refugee in Paris from embattled Spain, is exceedingly uneven but now and then powerful. In Fando et Lis the mystery is cruel. Who has doomed the two young lovers to be spiritually stillborn? Nomadic, they wander with a baby carriage holding the young heroine, the paralyzed Lis. The problem remains totally unsolved.

In Thieves' Carnival, a fantasy by Jean Anouilh, lovers, not star-crossed, fall afoul of the problematic nature of love itself. It is a beautiful play steeped in inconclusiveness. What is the mystery in its bones? It is everywhere and nowhere. There is no explanation, no outlet for baffled love. It goes on and on.

Why is there war? We know of no greater mystery. Jean Giraudoux's Tiger at the Gates confronts this age-old question. Giraudoux finds no solution. At the same time, in the character of Helen there is one slanted answer. Sheer eroticism burns. Helen, in her beauty, helps to provoke the Trojan War.

Einstein's closed universe and Beckett's desire to return to the womb are paradigms. Each is highly particular. Beckett's metaphor, visible in Endgame, is also a view of his dramatic universe. The two paradigms have something in common. The inner world of Beckett, the outer world of Einstein are analogous in ultimate meanings, though dissimilar in pristine shapes.

The nuclear bomb, symbol of modern danger, with its awesome dread, shocked Einstein with its potentialities for destructiveness. Beckett, Ionesco, and Arrabal, as well as the lesser-known Gabriel Cousin, have lived under the spell of atomic horror.

In his private life, Einstein fought doggedly for world peace. Jean Giraudoux, in Tiger at the Gates, intimated the consequences of juggling with local conflicts (a warning salutary for today). War arrives; the tiger is still at the gates. In The Madwoman of Chaillot, the author lets us see the mad ravages of the earth by exploiters of oil. The image is unmistakable; man will despoil his universe, in a stupid war of nonsense against unprotected harmony.

Einstein created a spatial universe in which drastic new principles held sway. Light curves. Space is dynamic. But much of it is unknown. In Alfred Jarry's wild farce, Ubu the King, the final destination of the conspirators is emptiness, empty space. Nul and void, néant: Ubu and his friends have no other true homeland. Unscientific, their odyssey is unheard of in modern drama. Ubu is a figure of pure bloodlust and carnage, made to live, as Jarry said pointedly, nowhere.

The Satin Slipper, by Paul Claudel, ranges through cosmic time and cosmic space. Claudel is a dramatic adventurer; somewhat comparable to today's explorers of space, he wants to encompass the universe with techniques of near-simultaneity. This sort of drama attacks the problems of space in a global sense. Time is more resistant. However, Claudel's play breaks conventions of temporality to evoke several different countries as scenes of the action with little regard to time.

Very differently, Guillaume Apollinaire's The Breasts of Tiresias (first played in 1917) defies space and time. Zanzibar, the comedy's supposed location, simultaneously evokes African climates, Paris, and a popular game played with dice. We are unsure about where things are happening. Temporally, a husband gives birth to more than 40,000 children, almost in the wink of an eye. We are baffled by time as well. The long and short of it is that Apollinaire sublimely miscast time and space, unlike traditionalistic theatre which preceded The Breasts of Tiresias.

Jean Cocteau's Orphée (1926)[9] features a hero who beats a path from earth to Hell. For him, it is relatively easy. He passes through a mirror, symbol of death. A friend and glazier, Heurtebise, hangs miraculously in mid-air. Halfway between ordinariness and the other worlds of spirits, Heurtebise is one of Cocteau's most unique characters. He has magic potential, cherished as art by Cocteau. Limitations of space vanish in a trice.

---

9 Jean Cocteau, Orphée (Paris: Stock, 1927) (ed. Jacques Guicharnaud) in Anthology of 20th Century French Theatre (New York-Paris: Paris Book Center, 1967).

The First Celestial Adventure of M. Antipyrine
(1916), by Tristan Tzara, teaches the bizarre uncertainty of drama itself.  In so doing, it seems to intimate
the fact that the universe is strangely wavering, uncertain.  One basis of science is ultimate uncertainty.
Heisenburg's principle of indeterminacy, involving the
impossibility of totally exact measurements of subatomic particles because of the disturbance caused by
the measuring instrument, is a cardinal rule of modern
physics.

Einstein said that the mystery of the universe was
its beauty.  Tzara and the Dada/surrealist poets tossed
logic and characterization, plot and locale, to the
winds.  Uncertainty and, sometimes, topsy-turvy disorder
are predominant.

Such is the theoretical grounding.  In practice,
on stage, it is not possible to evade order of some
kind.  So Dada characterizations are not without a certain degree of logical connection, even in the blurting
of nonsense syllables.  Uncertainty also breeds some
certainty.  Dada helped this strange anomaly along;
other playwrights followed, transfiguring Dada's discoveries.  The period 1905-1945 was acquainted with
Einstein, in France as in the United States.  He had
more popularity than any name in Western physics.

One of the most remarkable features of Einstein's
life was his championing of peace.  It was no doubt a
losing cause.  Yet he continued.  He made speech after
speech to denounce war.  Modern French playwrights have
developed viewpoints on the disastrous killings war
leaves.  A memorable satire is Fernando Arrabal's Picnic on the Battlefield (1959).  Who can say whether a
virulent drama of this kind, widely played in United
States' universities, will have more lasting effect than
Einstein's speeches?  Drama, because of its greater
durability, may well have more impact in the long run.

Gabriel Cousin's Le Drame du Fukuryu Maru (1960)
shows the terrifying results of American atomic fallout
on a group of Japanese fishermen in the Pacific.  It is
a human, searing indictment.  Few would be able to forget its havoc, its scarred bodies, and its implications,
once having seen or read the play.

Tiger at the Gates, by Jean Giraudoux (1935) is a
masked indictment.  War is the villain.  A tiger, armed

combat, is preparing destruction, waiting at the gate. Hector and Ulysses fight against the coming Trojan war. It comes. Giraudoux implies that despite diplomatic efforts of good will, there is a force unleashed in the world which defeats the peacemakers. War is inevitable; this is the tragedy.

A dizzying eclipse of time (Einsteinian in the sense that past, present, and future flow together) dominates Exit the King, by Eugène Ionesco (1963). King Béranger has lived for centuries; but now he must die. Time turns somersaults. It has reversals. Except for one fact: the doctor and his wife warn him that in a given number of minutes (is it the time left in the performance? It would seem so), his death will be a reality. Yes, this happens. Only after fanciful, well-tuned speeches in which the joy of past life is predominant.

Space, twin of time, as in Einstein, is fluid. Past feats, past reigning over his kingdom are hardly situated. Yet they have dramatic texture and potency. Treating death as foreboding, seen in advance, almost timeless, Exit the King incorporates Ionesco's own fears and his wonderful understanding of time/space interrelationships.

Jean Anouilh wrote a corrosive drama, Traveller without Luggage (1937)[11] on amnesia. The hero, Gaston, renounces his past, unbelievably. He had seduced his brother's wife and seriously injured one of his best friends. He throws the past away. A deus ex machina intervenes. A young British boy suddenly appears, offering him a home and family. Gaston rejects his own family, his sordid doings in the past, and welcomes the new adventure. He finally overthrows the hegemony of what he once did.

Experience and theory. Simplicity and economy. Einstein's working techniques, good sense in every way, should be made clear.

Modern French playwrights, working in a completely

---

[10] Jean Anouilh, Le Voyageur sans bagage (Traveller without Luggage) (Paris: Livre de Poche, 1958).

different medium, have created their own types of economy, sparseness, and transformed life. The drama, after all, is refracted experience, not theory. I have cited Beckett's Waiting for Godot, one of the most famous modern plays, read by a great many students in colleges and universities in Europe and America. Godot is bare, lean in its experimentation and much of its dialogue. It is deceptive. Its fame comes from its concision, razor-edged in meaning. To trick the cards, Beckett includes the well-known monologue of Lucky, twisted, contorted, deliberately enigmatic. It is an exception. Theatre is honed-down experience, rarified and ordered. There is no escape from that.

No one can define Fernando Arrabal's theatre. Cruelty is its hallmark. Why? No one has answered that sufficiently. The paralyzed Lis, pushed in a baby carriage by Fando, her lover, is a key heroine of Arrabal's. Symbolism is rampant. She is the wounded modern world. Fando's cruelty, simple and outright, is inexplicable. This symbolizes how a sick universe is evolving, fed on drugs and violence, seen and forecast by Arrabal.


In theory, perhaps, man can get rid of war. The motions we are now enacting, on stage as in the streets, denote something else.

It is obviously a tour de force to cite a group of modern French playwrights since Alfred Jarry (1896) as having presented analogies to the ideas of Alfred Einstein.

Taking this into consideration, I have tried to show analogous relationships in their works and Einstein's concepts. These partial correspondences exist. The problem is to be accurate in assessing the exact nature and degree of such relationships.

I have not meant to trace Einsteinian "influences" on modern French drama. Few if any of the dramatists I have analyzed have mentioned reading Einstein. Nor have they discussed his ideas in print, to the best of my knowledge. My study is not one of influences, but of rather distant yet clear-cut confrontations.

My findings surprised me. Why should they? As I have said, Einstein, Marx and Freud were the intellectu-

al talismans of their day.  If playwrights had not read
Einstein (whose writings are quite difficult), many had
heard of his theories, whether vaguely or definitely.
Henry-René Lenormand  staged Time is a Dream (1919).
Critics jumped on a bandwagon of mistaken evidence,
asserting that Lenormand was writing an Einsteinian
play about the relativity of time.  The truth was the
opposite.  Lenormand did not know the crux of Einstein's
theories.

Mysteriousness and beauty.  Peering into the universe, Einstein loved them.  His techniques for discovery revolutionized physics, as did his results.
Einstein was a name on learned persons' lips.  He was
called the most famous scientific man of his day.

French scenic authors, some of them following in
the strange footsteps of the devastating Alfred Jarry,
author of Ubu the King (1896), manipulated time, space
and motion in surprising ways.  Some of these theatrical creativities, by the very fact of belonging to
their intellectual ambiance, recalled Einstein's
theories.  Not replicas, they conserved their own na-
tures.  This is justice.  Few of the playwrights were
Einsteinian in essence.

They, too, sought the beauty of the mysterious.
Some plunged into the recondite:  e.g., Genet's harsh
drama, The Blacks.

What did these playwrights owe to Alfred Einstein?
His basic precepts of gravitation, time, light, speed,
space, and pre-atomic discovery were refracted, indirectly, into many of the outstanding plays of the
French stage after 1896.  Analogies are perceptible.
These are phenomena of intellectual, prismatic thought,
passed on through the Einsteinian atmosphere.

SOME OF EINSTEIN'S CONCEPTS

I. SPACE AND TIME

Space and time are forms of intuition. Einstein showed this. They "can no more be divorced from consciousness than can our concepts of color, shape, and size. Space has no objective reality except as an order or arrangement of the objects we perceive in it, and time has no independent existence apart from the order of events by which we measure it."[1]

To describe the motion of a particle or wave the concepts of time and distance are used. These concepts are left undefined as intuitive, with universally understood meanings.

A continuum is an area that is continuous and self-same. In relativity mechanics new views of the nature of time and space were developed by Einstein and others. These ideas came from thought experiments involving the description of events that included the position and time at which this event occurs.

II. LIGHT

In the early nineteenth century it was generally agreed that light is a wave phenomenon. This required that there must be some material medium in which the waves could travel. This hypothetical and controversial medium was given the name ether. A great deal of effort was made to measure ether drift, that is the speed of light in different directions because of the orbital motion of the earth.

The Michelson-Morley experiments (1881 and later)

---

[1] Lincoln Barnett, The Universe and Dr. Einstein (New York: Bantam, 1974), p. 19.

were reported to be entirely negative with regard to an ether drift. Therefore, it became clearer that there is no ether. Einstein concluded that the speed of light in empty space must be identical in all directions, independent of the motion of source or observer. This fact led Einstein to his development of the Special Theory of Relativity.


III.  THE SPECIAL THEORY OF RELATIVITY


This theory made some simple predictions of great importance, such as the impossibility of a particle speed greater than the speed of light, and the interconvertibility of matter and energy. The basic studies discussed in this theory are:  (1) Relations between time and distance measured by two observers moving with respect to each other (the Lorentz Transformation); (2) The Lorentz Contraction. An object moving at high speed (approaching the speed of light) will appear to a stationary observer to suffer a contraction; a meter stick passing an observer with a speed 60% the speed of light would appear to be only 80 cm long; (3) Time Dilation. A clock moving with a speed approaching the speed of light would appear to a stationary observer to record time much slower than ordinarily. For example, a radioactive particle travelling with a speed of 60% the speed of light would have its half-life increased by 25%. (4) The Twin Paradox. Space travelers will not age as fast as twin brothers on earth. If a space traveler twin brother could move with the speed of light he would not age at all in comparison with his twin on earth! Time slows down for a space traveler. (5) Mass-Energy Relation. Einstein proposed that there is a connection between matter and energy that is represented by the famous formula $E = mc^2$. When a particle of matter is converted to energy (matter into radiation) a tremendous amount of energy is released. This is the basis of nuclear bombs.

MASS

SPEED                                              186,000 mi/sec

Einstein interpreted the negative result of the Michelson-Morley experiments to show that only relative velocity can be measured, not absolute velocity. His special theory of relativity considered only reference systems moving at a constant velocity relative to each other.

This theory was based on two postulates:

(a) In either of two reference systems moving with constant velocity relative to each other, the laws of physical phenomena are the same. In these laws, there is no reference to an ether.

(b) The velocity of light in empty space is the same for all observers and is independent of the light source relative to the observer. When two events take place simultaneously at different locations it is impossible to say which of the two precedes the other or to say that they occur simultaneously.

IV. THE GENERAL THEORY OF RELATIVITY

This deals primarily with the theory of gravitation (1915). Example: A man in an elevator which is falling completely free. The man observes that he appears to be "weightless." If he were hanging from a spring balance it would read zero. This can be interpreted by the man in two ways: (a) he may think that gravity has been turned off so that he is not attracted to the earth or (b) he may conclude that the elevator is moving with "the acceleration g" (32 ft/sec$^2$) and he is moving with the elevator.

Another example: An astronaut in a circular orbit around the earth appears to be "weightless." Actually, he is being accelerated toward the earth with the acceleration g, as a result of gravity. But there is no way for an observer in the space station to distinguish, by means of experiments in the station, between his situation and one he might perform in a train moving with constant velocity in a region that had zero gravity. Technically this means that there is no way to distinguish between a gravitational field and a region in an accelerated reference system.

The heart of the general theory is the hypothesis

that an accelerated reference system and a gravitational field are really two aspects of the same thing. This is called the "Principle of Equivalence."

There are several effects predicted by the general theory that are not included in the special theory. A familiar one is the bending of light in a strong gravitational field. This was observed during an eclipse of the sun as light from a distant star was attracted toward the sun. (Very small effect and results difficult to observe.) (a) Gravitational Field. In Newtonian mechanics a basic postulate is that there is a force of attraction between every particle in the universe and every other particle. This force is called gravitation and the region between the two particles is a gravitational field.

In the general theory of relativity a "pseudo-gravitational" force is postulated whenever an object is accelerated in a reference system. For example, when a space ship is blasted off, an astronaut has the impression that gravity has been increased (sometimes 5-8 times that of ordinary earth gravity). No physics experiment performed inside the space ship could tell the observer whether the gravitational field of the earth had suddenly increased or whether the space ship was accelerating with respect to the earth. (b) Measurements in spectroscopy have shown that the galaxies at a distance of five billion "light years" are receding from us with about half the speed of light. This recession is measured by the "red shift," that is the wave lengths of light are observed to be longer ("redder") than that from atoms that are at rest relative to the earth.

If one calculated back in time, he could conclude that all the galaxies in the universe were crowded together in our space about 10-15 billion years ago. With this enormous condensation of matter, the laws of physics would predict that there would be a gigantic explosion of the condensed matter. Hence the receding galaxies might correspond to the pieces of an exploding grenade. This is the "big bang theory" of the expanding universe.

(c) The Mass-Energy Equation, $E = mc^2$. One of the best understood and demonstrated features of the Special Theory of Relativity is the theory that mass and energy are really two aspects of the same thing. Matter can be

transmuted into energy and vice-versa. The obvious
example is the nuclear bomb, where matter is converted
into energy. In a photoelectric cell, light is converted into the energy of an ejected electron.

(d) Gravity Waves. Einstein tried unsuccessfully
to develop theories linking gravity and electromagne-
tism. For fundamental-particle interactions gravity
is of no significance. But for the large-scale structure of the universe gravitational interaction is
highly significant. Current theories of such interactions employ non-euclidean geometries that are highly
mathematical and cannot be described in non-technical
terms.

(e) Photons and Quantum Theory. In 1905 Einstein
suggested that radiant energy not only is emitted and
absorbed in whole numbers of quanta (Planck Quantum
Theory) but also the radiation is propagated through
space as photons, moving with the speed of light. This
extension of the quantum theory implies a modification
of the wave theory of light in favor of a particle
theory. There is a dual nature of waves and particles.
In simplistic terms a beam of light can be considered
as a particle called a photon.

(f) Equivalence. The heart of the general theory
of relativity is the hypothesis that an accelerated
frame of reference (coordinate system) and a gravitational field are really two aspects of the same thing.
One cannot experimentally distinguish between them;
therefore it makes no sense to try to consider them as
different. This, as I have said, is called the Principle of Equivalence. If one accepts this theory he
is led to the assumption that space is in general non-
euclidean.

(g) One concept arising from this theory is the
idea of a "black hole." This is the region in which a
massive star has collapsed to the point where its
density is so enormous (a thousand million times that
of water) that gravitational interactions prevent any
radiation from escaping from the black hole.

Einstein had a new vision of the space-time continuum. In his general theory of relativity, the
space-time continuum is not a euclidean continuum.

105

Space is a three-dimension continuum...Similarly, the world of physical phenomena called 'world' by Minkowski is naturally four-dimensional in the space-time sense. The 'world' is in this sense also a continuum."[2]

Closed spaces without limits are conceivable. From amongst these, the spherical space (and the elliptical) excel in simplicity, since all points on it are equivalent.[3]

It may be mentioned that there is yet another kind of curved space: 'elliptical space.' It can be regarded as a curved space in which the two 'counterpoints' are identical (indistinguishable from each other).

Space is curved. Along with Einstein's startling discovery that a ray of light is bent as it passes a gravitational object, this is most remarkable. Space and time are intimately related and depend on the relative motion of observers.

The geometry of space is changing with time. Thus, the dynamic universe as seen by Einstein takes over controls of time and space. Everything is in flux, in constant change. Defining time or space totally once and for all is impossible.

## COLOR

Colors, as we perceive them, are relative; they depend on light and shade, on emotions. Similarly, temperatures. Two bodies with equal temperatures do not contain equal amounts of heat. Each substance has its individual heat capacity. A dive into the ocean: there is no single definite temperature of the water on parts of the skin. It is all relative.

---

[2] Albert Einstein, Relativity: the Special and General Theory (New York: Crown, 1961), p. 55.

[3] Ibid., p. 112.

Again, we must take care to separate terms useful in physics and those we employ in everyday parlance. Yet the terms may merge. Heat, for example. Body temperature can be measured scientifically. But it is always relative to pertinent conditions: outside temperature, the internal body's workings, emotions. In a very strict sense, obviously, Einsteinian relativity is inapplicable to literary artefacts.

The average person is amazed to learn that a ray of light is bent when it passes a gravitational body. Where are our former absolutes? According to Einstein,

the curvature of light rays required by the General Theory of Relativity is only exceedingly small for the gravitational fields at our disposal in practice, its estimated magnitude for light rays passing the sun at grazing incidence is nevertheless 1/7 second of arc.[4]

## MORE ON TIME AND SPACE

Our sense experiences have led us into a false idea of time. We forget that the notion of time itself comes initially in our everyday experience as we witness sequences of events taking place in one locality (cf. a tennis match) rather than in all of space.[5]

As we see time in everyday terms, it is often clearly relative. When one takes a short flight by air from Lawrence, Kansas to Kansas City in a small commuter plane, events determine whether time seems relatively long or relatively short. Space also seems relative.

Einstein had said, "The notion of time itself arises initially in our everyday experience by watching sequences of events happening in one locality, rather than in all of space."[6]

---

[4] Albert Einstein, op. cit., p. 75.
[5] Cf. Gerald Holton, "Constructing a Theory: Einstein's Model," The American Scholar, vol. 48, no. 3 (Summer, 1979), p. 310.
[6] Cited in Ibid., p. 310.

Time dilation is another consequence of special relativity; according to this phenomenon, if two observers are moving at constant velocity relative to each other, it will appear to each that the other's clocks have been slowed down. This affects the concept of simultaneity.[7]

Space-time is a difficult concept. Hermann Minkowski gave a mathematical formulation of the special theory of relativity. He proceeds from the idea that an event is specified by four coordinates, three spatial coordinates and one time coordinate. These coordinates define a four-dimensional space. A particle motion can be described by a curve in this space, which is called Minkowski space-time.[8]

The special theory of relativity is concerned with relative motion between non-accelerated frames of reference. The second part of the theory of relativity, published in 1915 and known as the general theory of relativity, deals with general relative motion between accelerated frames of reference.

In accelerated frames of reference certain "fictitious" forces are observed, such as the centrifugal and Coriolis forces found in rotating systems. These are known as "fictitious" forces because they disappear when the observer transforms to a non-accelerated system.

For example, to an observer in a car rounding a bend at constant speed objects in the car appear to suffer a force acting outwards. To an observer outside the car this is simply their tendency to continue moving in a straight line. The inertia of the objects is seen to produce a fictitious force and the observer can distinguish between non-inertial (accelerated) and inertial (non-accelerated) frames of reference.

[7] The Penguin Dictionary of Physics, ed. Valerie H. Pitt (Harmondsworth: Penguin, 1978), p. 325.

[8] Cf. Ibid., p. 324.

To the observer in the car, all the objects are given the same acceleration irrespective of their mass.  This implies a connection between the fictitious forces arising from accelerated systems and forces due to gravity, where the acceleration produced is independent of the mass...

A further principle used in the General Theory is that the laws of mechanics are the same in inertial and non-inertial frames of reference.

The equivalence between a gravitational field and the fictitious forces in non-inertial systems can be expressed by using Riemannian space-time, which differs from the space-time of the Special Theory (Minkowski space-time).

In special relativity the motion of a particle that is not acted on by any forces is represented by a straight line in Minkowski space-time.

In general relativity, using Riemanninan space-time, the motion is represented by a line that is no longer straight (in the Euclidean sense) but is the line giving the shortest distance.  Such a line is called a geodesic.

Thus space-time is said to be curved.

The fact that gravitational effects occur near masses is introduced by the postulate that the presence of matter produces this curvature of space-time."9


Space-time, therefore, is curved.  The presence of mass which can have effect on it causes this curvature. Lines curve.  This is an astonishing fact, curiously though indirectly discernible in modern French theatre.

---

9 Ibid., p. 324.

109

BIBLIOGRAPHY


BOOKS ON SCIENCE

Isaac Asimov, Please Explain (New York, Dell, 1973).

Isaac Asimov, The Collapsing Universe: The Story of
    Black Holes (New York:  Pocket Books, 1978).

Lincoln Barnett, The Universe and Dr. Einstein (New York:
    Bantam, 1974).

Arthur Beiser (ed.), The World of Physics (New York:
    McGraw-Hill, 1960).

Jeremy Bernstein, Einstein (Harmondsworth:  Penguin,
    1973).

J. Bronowski, The Ascent of Man (Boston:  Little, Brown,
    1973).

J. Bronowski, The Origins of Knowledge and Imagination
    (New Haven:  Yale, 1978).

Nigel Calder, Einstein's Universe (New York:  Viking,
    1979).

Ronald W. Clark, Einstein:  The Life and Times (New
    York:  Avon, 1972).

James B. Conant, Modern Science and Modern Man (New
    York:  Doubleday Anchor, 1953).

Albert Einstein, Ideas and Opinions (New York:  Crown,
    1954).

Albert Einstein, Relativity:  The Special and General
    Theory (New York:  Crown, 1961).

Albert Einstein, What I Believe, 1930.

Albert Einstein, Autobiographical Notes (translated and

edited by Paul Arthur Schilpp) (Chicago: Open Court, 1979).

Martin Gardner, The Relativity Explosion (New York: Vintage, 1976).

Jagdish Mehra (ed.), The Physicist's Conception of Nature (Boston: Reidel, 1973).

Lloyd, Motz, The Universe: Its Beginning and End (New York: Scribner's, 1975).

Valerie H. Pitt, (ed.) The Penguin Dictionary of Physics (Harmondsworth: Penguin, 1978).

B. K. Ridley, Time, Space and Things (Harmondsworth: Penguin, 1976).

Bertrand Russell, The ABC of Relativity (New York: Mentor, 1969).

Carl Seelig, Albert Einstein: A Documentary Biography (London, 1956).

Gerald Tauber (ed.), Albert Einstein's Theory of General Relativity (New York, Crown, 1979).


BOOKS ON FRENCH DRAMA


Deirdre Bair, Beckett (New York: Harcourt Brace Jovanovich, 1978).

Michael Benedikt and George E. Wellwarth, eds., Modern French Theatre (New York: Dutton, 1966).

Simone Benmussa, Ionesco (Paris: Seghers, 1966).

Tom Bishop (ed.), L'avant-garde théâtrale (Lexington, Mass.: Heath, 1970).

Tom Driver, Jean Genet (New York: Columbia University Press, 1966).

Wolfgang Bernard Fleischmann, ed., Encyclopedia of World
    Literature in the 20th Century (New York: Ungar,
    1967).

John Gassner and Edward Quinn, eds., The Reader's Ency-
    clopedia of World Drama (New York: Crowell, 1969).

Bernard Gille, Arrabal (Paris: Seghers, 1970).

Jacques Guicharnaud, ed., Anthology of 20th Century
    French Theater (Paris-New York: Paris Book Center,
    1967).

Jacques Guicharnaud, Modern French Theatre (New Haven:
    Yale University Press, 1961).

William H. Harris and Judith S. Levey, eds., The New
    Columbia Encyclopedia (New York and London: Colum-
    bia University Press, 1975).

René Lalou, Le Théâtre en France depuis 1900 (Paris:
    Presses Universitaires de France, 1961).

Robert G. Marshall and Frederic C. St. Aubyn, eds.,
    Trois pièces surréalistes (New York: Appleton-Cen-
    tury-Crofts, 1969).

J. H. Matthews, Theatre in Dada and Surrealism (Syra-
    cuse: Syracuse University Press, 1974).

Leonard Cabell Pronko, The World of Jean Anouilh (Berke-
    ley and Los Angeles: University of California Press,
    1968).

Oreste Pucciani, The French Theater since 1930 (Boston:
    Ginn, 1954).

Marcel Raymond, From Baudelaire to Surrealism (New York:
    Wittenborn, 1950).

S. A. Rhodes, ed., The Contemporary French Theater (New
    York: Crofts, 1947).

Geneviève Serreau, Histoire du 'nouveau théâtre' (Paris:
    Gallimard, 1966).

Roger Shattuck, The Banquet Years (Garden City, N.Y.:
    Anchor, 1958).

113

# FRENCH PLAYS AND OTHERS

Jean Anouilh, Le voyageur sans bagages [Traveler without Baggage] et Le bal des voleurs [Thieves' Carnival] (Paris: Livre de Poche, 1958).

Fernando Arrabal, Fando et Lis [Fando and Lis], in Thé-âtre I (Paris: Christian Bourgois, 1958).

Fernando Arrabal, Pique-nique en campagne [Picnic on the Battlefield], in Panorama du théâtre nouveau, Le théâtre de la dérision, Jacques G. Benay and Reinhard Kuhn, eds., (New York: Appleton-Century-Crofts, 1967).

Fernando Arrabal, Le Tricycle, in Théâtre (Paris: Julliard, 1961).

Samuel Beckett, En attendant Godot [Waiting for Godot], Germaine Brée and Eric Schoenfeld, eds., (New York: Macmillan, 1964).

Samuel Beckett, Endgame (New York: Grove, 1958).

Paul Claudel, Le Soulier de Satin, [The Satin Slipper], Marcel Girard, ed., (Paris: Classiques Larousse, 1956).

Gabriel Cousin, Le Drame du Fukuryu Maru (Paris: Gallimard, 1960).

Jean Genet, Les Nègres [The Blacks] (Décines, France: Marc Barbezat, 1960).

Jean Giraudoux, La Guerre de Troie n'aura pas lieu [Tiger at the Gates] (Paris: Classiques Larousse, 1959).

Jean Giraudoux, Intermezzo [The Enchanted] (Paris: Grasset, 1933).

Eugène Ionesco, Amédée ou Comment s'en debarrasser [Amédée] in Théâtre I (Paris: Gallimard, 1954).

Eugène Ionesco, La Cantatrice chauve [The Bald Soprano] in Théâtre I (Paris: Gallimard, 1954).

114

Eugène Ionesco, La Colère, in Théâtre III (Paris: Galli-
    mard, 1963).

Eugène Ionesco, La Leçon [The Lesson], in Théâtre I
    (Paris: Gallimard, 1954).

Eugène Ionesco, Le Roi se meurt [Exit the King] (Paris:
    Gallimard, 1963).

Alfred Jarry, Ubu Roi [Ubu the King], in Tout Ubu, Mau-
    rice Saillet, ed., (Paris: Librairie Générale
    Francaise, 1962).


OTHER PLAYS


Friedrich Dürrenmatt, The Physicists (New York, Grove,
    1962).

William Shakespeare, Hamlet, Willard Farnham, ed.
    (Baltimore: Penguin, 1969).

William Shakespeare, King Lear, Francis Fergusson, ed.
    (New York: Dell, 1960).


MEMOIRS


Eugène Ionesco, Notes and Counternotes (New York: Grove,
    1974).


ARTICLES


Tristan Tzara, "Guillaume Apollinaire," Dada, no. 2,
    December 1917.

Atlantic Monthly, November 1945 and November, 1947 (As told to Raymond Swing.)

Kenneth F. Weaver and James P. Blair, "The Incredible Universe," National Geographic, May 1974, Vol. 145, no. 5, pp. 589-625.

"The Year of Dr. Einstein," Time, February 19, 1979.

John H. Wilhelm, "A Singular Man," Quest, April 1979, p. 33.

Carl Sagan, "The Amniotic Universe," Atlantic Monthly, April 1979, p. 45.

Gerald Holtin, "Constructing a Theory: Einstein's Model," The American Scholar, vol. 48, no. 3 (Summer, 1979), pp. 309-340.

"Saturn," Science 80, November/December 1979.

Dietrick E. Thomsen, "Personality, Place, and Physics," Science News, vol. 115, 1979, p. 212.

Scientific American, January 1980, Vol. 242, no. 1.